THE MANAGEMENT OF POLICE SPECIALIZED TACTICAL UNITS

ABOUT THE AUTHORS

Dr. Tomas C. Mijares joined the Criminal Justice faculty at Southwest Texas State University after retiring from the Detroit Police Department as a sergeant in 1991. He spent the majority of his career as a sergeant in patrol supervision and tactical operations. He earned his Master's degree from the University of Detroit and his Ph.D. from the University of Michigan. Dr. Mijares serves as a member of the Training Advisory Committee for the Texas Tactical Police Officers Association. His research findings in police management and criminal investigation have been published in several journals and presented at conferences of the Academy of Criminal Justice Sciences.

Ronald M. McCarthy retired from the Los Angeles Police Department after a distinguished career in tactical operations. He received the Medal of Valor in 1975 and was recognized for courageous action during the rescue of hostages in 1983. He was named Police Officer of the Year in 1976 and received the NTOA's Award of Excellence in 1990. In 1995 he received the All American Hero Award. Since retirement he has served as a tactical consultant to the Department of Energy, the Department of Justice, the International Association of Chiefs of Police, and the National Tactical Officers Association.

Dr. David B. Perkins is a member of the Criminal Justice faculty at Southwest Texas State University. A graduate of Lamar University and the University of Texas School of Law, Dr. Perkins has served a combined 25 years in municipal prosecution and judicial functions. His scholarly interests are in the area of substantive and procedural criminal law, constitutional issues, and civil liability of public agencies. His research has been published at several journals and presented in national conferences.

THE MANAGEMENT OF POLICE SPECIALIZED TACTICAL UNITS

By

TOMAS C. MIJARES, Ph.D.
Department of Criminal Justice
Southwest Texas State University
San Marcos, Texas

RONALD M. McCARTHY
Sergeant, Los Angeles Police Department (Retired)
Los Angeles, California

and

DAVID B. PERKINS, J.D.
Department of Criminal Justice
Southwest Texas State University
San Marcos, Texas

Charles C Thomas
PUBLISHER • LTD.
SPRINGFIELD • ILLINOIS • U.S.A.

Published and Distributed Throughout the World by

CHARLES C THOMAS · PUBLISHER, LTD.
2600 South First Street
Springfield, Illinois 62794-9265

©*2000 by* CHARLES C THOMAS · PUBLISHER, LTD.

ISBN 0-398-07069-5 (cloth)
ISBN 0-398-07070-9 (paper)

Library of Congress Catalog Card Number: 00-027308

With THOMAS BOOKS *careful attention is given to all details of manufacturing
and design. It is the Publisher's desire to present books that are satisfactory as to their
physical qualities and artistic possibilities and appropriate for their particular use.*
THOMAS BOOKS *will be true to those laws of quality that assure a good name
and good will.*

Printed in the United States of America
CR-R-3

Library of Congress Cataloging-in-Publication Data

Mijares, Tomas C.
    The management of police specialized tactical units / by Tomas
C. Mijares, Ronald M. McCarthy, David B. Perkins.
        p.   cm.
    Includes bibliographical references and index.
    ISBN 0-398-07069-5 (cloth) -- ISBN 0-398-07070-9 (paper)
    1. Police--Special weapons and tactics units. 2. Police--United States--
Special weapons and tactics units. I. McCarthy, Ronald M. II. Perkins,
David B. III. Title.

HV8080.S64 M54 2000
363.2'32--dc21

                                                    00-027308

CONTRIBUTING AUTHOR

Dr Michael T. England earned his Ph.D. from the University of Tennessee. A former news reporter, Dr. England is currently a member of the Department of Mass Communications at Southwest Texas State University.

INTRODUCTION

Professional police supervisors and administrators are responsible for more than enforcing the law and maintaining order. They must ensure that the officers who perform these functions do so within socially and legally established parameters while remaining within the constraints of a budget. Under various theories of civil liability, the police supervisor, administrator, and ultimately, the chief executive of the law enforcement agency may also assume legal responsibility for the actions of their subordinates. The corresponding ability of subordinate law enforcement personnel to perform assigned tasks within the established guidelines has a direct impact on the careers of their supervisors.

Several books have already been written about special weapons and tactics for street police officers to assist them in the development of the skills needed in the performance of their duties. Most of these books have been directed toward individual officer performance in the field and are often modifications of military field manuals and standard operating procedures of state and local police departments. Other discussions of emergency and tactical management have focused on the field management of the actual crisis.

This book is not meant to be a manual on how to become a better tactical officer nor is it intended to be a checklist of procedures to be followed at the scene of a critical incident. Skill-based training of this sort is in a continuous state of refinement and is readily available through several sources mentioned in Chapters Five and Six. Certainly the book should not be construed as an inhibiting set of legal proscriptions designed to limit the ability of tactical units to perform their duties. Just as the net effect of the landmark Supreme Court decision of *Miranda v. Arizona* was to strengthen the quality of criminal prosecution, thereby increasing the conviction rate of offenders, the court cases cited here should be regarded as information to improve organizational quality and operational effectiveness.

The material that follows is different from its predecessors because it is written with a proactive emphasis. It is incumbent on management, from team leaders and immediate supervisors to the organizational chief executive officer who is forced to be sensitive to the demands placed on the agency by society, by the legal system and by their own budgets to follow a proactive approach. This sort of approach is initiated through an identification of potential issues long before the perpetrator initiates any criminal activity. Largely following Luther Gulick's (1937) classic description of the elements of management,[1] this book will attempt to explain the steps for developing and maintaining a realistic, effective response to increasing levels of sophisticated violent crime. It will discuss the social and political matters that must be defined, identified, and settled prior to the implementation of any substantive or procedural change in tactical policy. This book is, thus, more concerned with the advanced management functions of developing organizational structure, policies, personnel, and resources needed in the resolution of critical incidents. The book will also discuss media relations, relations with other criminal justice agencies, and intradepartmental politics.

It would be insufficient merely to answer the basic questions about who should create a tactical capability within a law enforcement agency, what must be done to achieve this capability, where to find the equipment and expertise needed to become operational, when the tactical unit must be mobilized and exercised, and how this capability relates to the overall police mission. As each issue is identified and examined, an attempt is made to go beyond previous texts by explaining the organizational rationale for each decision.

Another recurring theme found in this book will be the responsibility of the law enforcement agency and its supervisory and administrative personnel to follow legal guidelines in the formation and operation of the tactical unit. The agencies that currently maintain or in the future will seek to form tactical units are as diverse and fragmented as our entire criminal justice system. In turn, such diversity means that there exists a broad range of disparate legal principles, depending on the jurisdictional origins of a particular agency.

---

1. Planning, organizing, staffing, directing, coordinating, reporting, and budgeting.

The entire range of possible jurisdiction-specific theories upon which liability claims against field officers, supervisors, and governmental bodies might be predicated is beyond the scope of this work but should be examined separately by police administrators for their own jurisdictions. The same is true for various defenses to liability that may exist. However, generally speaking, causes of action founded in intentional wrongdoing, negligence, and so-called constitutional torts are somewhat common concerns (Mijares and Perkins, 1994).

This work will, therefore, present certain legal precedents as described in appellate judicial opinions to study relevant issues as they might arise in the courts. These appellate court opinions are included in legal discussion not because they represent the only, the best, or the majority view of the law, but because on their facts or within their texts they appear to be informative. Additional commentary derived from literary review will at times likewise accompany the cases offered.

This book also makes extensive use of actual field examples to illustrate various points. In so doing, another important difference between previous publications and this book is identifiable. Authors of earlier presentations of literature related to tactical operations have primarily used case studies of successful operations as examples of proper procedures. Much can be discovered by analysis of less successful incident resolutions as well. It would be misleading and an exercise in futility to claim that only one method is appropriate for all circumstances or even any given single situation. Political, social, and technical conditions change on a daily basis, and a panacea is not possible or even desirable. The principles developed in this examination allow and actually encourage adjustment to change.

This book will further serve a final purpose. The model of management suggested herein can be applied to other areas of law enforcement. Whether the area of attention is vice crimes, traffic law enforcement, or the investigation of organized crime activity, the law enforcement manager is confronted daily with the same managerial issues addressed in this text.

ACKNOWLEDGMENTS

The authors wish to thank the following people for their patience, assistance, support, and suggestions throughout the entire project of preparing this text. We sincerely apologize for any omissions.

Our wives, Janet Mijares, Sandra McCarthy, and Ruthie Perkins
Dr. Ron Becker
Shannon Couch
Donald Drake
Mike Finley
Gregory Garvelli
Georgen Guerreor
Mike Hillman
Dr. Victor Kappeler
Dr. Dave Klinger
John Kolman
Dr. Harvey Kushner
Evan Marshall
Dr. Gordon E. Martin
Dr. Wayman Mullins
Dr. Maxwell Murphy
Norman Sieloff
Gerald Solai
Joe Soloman
Marcus L. "Sandy" Wall

CONTENTS

THE MANAGEMENT OF POLICE SPECIALIZED TACTICAL UNITS

Chapter One

THE HISTORY AND MISSION OF
SPECIALIZED POLICE TACTICAL UNITS

Several events in police history have demonstrated how law enforcement agencies at every level are at times too poorly prepared, organized, trained, and equipped to cope with an increasingly more violent and sophisticated criminal element. The concept of "special events" is difficult to define with any degree of precision. Special events are those events which are beyond the normal preparation and capability of standard patrol procedures and resources. These events include, but are not limited to, sniper incidents, barricaded subjects, hostage seizures, and dignitary protection situations. Although not every special event in American law enforcement has been as newsworthy as the M.O.V.E. confrontation in Philadelphia or the shootout between the Symbionese Liberation Army and the Los Angeles Police Department's Special Weapons and Tactics (SWAT) Unit, the increasing frequency and relative magnitude of events such as these are realities that must be addressed by the professional police administrator and by the elected officials to whom he or she must report.

CONVENTIONAL PATTERNS OF AMERICAN LAW
ENFORCEMENT [1]

Traditional methods of American law enforcement have centered around the beat cop making rounds on foot and taking the appropri-

---

1. Information for this section was developed through an oral history of law enforcement provided by retired police officers James Hillary (Grand Rapids Police Department) and James R. Tait (Detroit Police Department)

ate action through initiative and with limited resources. Backup assistance and radio calls to the station for advice were technically impossible until the relatively recent times of the middle twentieth century. Specialized response capabilities were initially limited to horse-mounted police officers and were later improved by the advent of the automobile and the "Flying Squads" of major city detective bureaus.

Labor unrest during the 1930s demonstrated the need for specialized police units possessing the means for immediate deployment, containment and arrest capabilities to deal with unusual circumstances such as barricaded suspects, demonstrations, strikes and other forms of unrest in a rapidly changing society. Racially charged incidents during the 1940s and later during the 1960s further demonstrated this need. However, the units that were developed were limited in their ability to perform these tasks.

With the exception of the New York Police Department's Emergency Services Unit for rescue operations, extraordinary circumstances were met with stop-gap measures. A physically large officer with an eagerness and ability to use force may have been the first selected for these special assignments. But the personnel selected for these circumstances were usually chosen on the basis of immediate availability instead of their training and demonstrated ability. Normally they received only an *ad hoc* status for a particular incident. As a result, the ranks and response time of the remaining patrol forces were depleted, and the more routine tasks of police work received a secondary priority or were ignored altogether. Members of these temporary task forces often had not worked together as a unit and almost never trained together. Consequently, these temporary units lacked the cohesiveness and coordination necessary to function properly as a unit. This lack of training also often led to an indiscriminate, undisciplined, and unaccountable use of force.

As police administrators recognized the need to maintain unit integrity for these events, specialized units were developed. Often given excitement-generating names such as the "Riot Squad" (many cities) or the "Commando Unit" (Detroit), these units generally operated on a part-time basis, whereby the officers assigned were mobilized and united only on an as-needed basis and returned to their regularly scheduled duties upon completion of the incident. Despite the assumption of elitism in the creation and maintenance of these units, the following shortcomings were identified by the National Commission on Law Observation and Enforcement:[2]

1. The selection process for most police appointments and assignments was often based on nepotism and favoritism. Any other criteria were based on officers' physical size, an estimate of their willingness and ability to use force, and/or personal possession of specialized equipment such as a high-powered rifle with a telescope.

2. Training was irregular, inconsistent, and incomplete. As a result, a greater amount of force was used than what may have been necessary. Until the recommendations made by the Commission were made operational, training had emphasized meeting force with increased force. Thus, any subsequent increase in resistance by the criminal perpetrator was simply met with an even greater increase in force by responding police personnel. Little, if any, attention was directed toward the containment, control, and de-escalation of a volatile situation through the use of negotiation, superior technology, or any of the other force-reducing tactics.

3. No continuous and concerted effort was made in large departments to integrate these units with other sections of the police departments.

4. Little research was conducted to find improvements to existing techniques and technology. Except for the advent of motorized vehicles and primitive radios, law enforcement technology had not changed appreciably since the nineteenth century. Communications beyond the station house were limited to a select few radio-equipped patrol cars which were initially only capable of reception. Weaponry was limited to a revolver, the shotgun (usually a double-barrel), the Thompson submachine gun, and the Winchester Model 94 rifle. Since the individual officer on the beat during these years was still very similar to the nineteenth -century counterpart, tactics and techniques were relatively unchanged and largely dependent on individual ability to employ force.

5. Specific department orders were not developed to define the deployment procedures to be followed by specialized units. The lines

---

2. In 1931 the National Commission on Law Observation and Enforcement, commonly referred to as the Wickersham Commission, was charged with the responsibility of reporting on the enforcement of the Eighteenth Amendment (Prohibition). Its overall conclusion was that Prohibition was not being enforced because it was an unenforceable task placed on American law enforcement. The Commission's 14-volume series of reports probed deeply into the American criminal justice system to offer the causes and effects of the situation and to suggest possible ameliorative efforts (Bopp & Schultz, 1972).

of authority, responsibility, accountability, and communications were obscure. Inefficiency was the rule rather than the exception. For many reasons the command structures usually stayed at arm's length from these units. Further muddying the waters of accountability and control, this lack of administrative fortitude led to the creation of rogue units and to misuse because their specialized duties were not fully understood by department executives. When they were used, these units often assumed roles as strike breakers or to keep minorities "in their place."

The situation did not change measurably through the 1940s, 1950s, and even beyond. For example, the forceful response of these specialized units to the protests of the college students of the 1960s was similar to the responses directed toward the labor protests of the 1930s.

AN INCREASE IN VIOLENCE IN A MORE COMPLEX SOCIETY

From the middle and late 1960s and early 1970s to the present, social and technical factors have been at work to change the complexion of law enforcement in general and tactical policing in particular. First, the war in Viet Nam and other conflicts resulted in a quantum increase in the number and variety of weapons available for law enforcement applications. Unfortunately, criminal elements throughout the world had (and continue to have) access to the same technology without the legal, social, and economic constraints endured by law enforcement agencies (Dobson and Payne, 1982). The huge operating budgets enjoyed by organized crime, particularly the elements involved in illegal drug trafficking and international terrorist operations, have produced a new breed of criminal whose weapons equal and usually surpass those of modern military and police forces. Their ruthless nature indicates that they have no reluctance to employ such weapons indiscriminately. Often purchased through legitimate sources, their armories include fully automatic rifles, rocket launchers, submachine guns, fragmentation grenades, and myriad explosives and detonating devices.

Second, America's space exploration program and its by-products have also had an impact on the technology of law enforcement and criminality. Limited space for orbiting payloads resulted in smaller, more efficient radio communications systems. Land-line callboxes and one-way radios in police cars were expanded to full two-way communications and were later improved by the PREP (Portable Radio Equipped Patrolman) radio. Originally weighing approximately five pounds each with a one-channel capacity and very limited operational range, portable two-way radios have now been improved to include multiple channels, scrambling and cross-district interphase capabilities and hands-free operation. It is especially useful for today's tactical officer to use a device slightly larger than a deck of playing cards for radio communication. Where law enforcement had traditionally been dependent on the unplanned and unrelated efforts of patrol officers acting individually, the improvement in communications now allows all involved law enforcement officers the opportunity to coordinate their efforts more effectively in surveillance, pursuits, high-risk warrant service, tactical operations, and other activities that optimally require several individuals to act as a unit.

Third, the frequency and magnitude of special threats have increased beyond the imagination of the beat cop of a few decades ago. Regardless of the size of a law enforcement agency's jurisdiction, it is extremely naive for a police administrator to ignore the possibility of extreme violence. History has already shown that these events are not limited by demographic and geographic factors. The Texas Tower incident in Austin, the Howard Johnson motel incident in New Orleans, the McDonald's Restaurant massacre in San Ysidro, California, and the fatal shooting of 23 customers in a central Texas restaurant are disturbing reminders of how a well-armed individual can easily and quickly inflict unspeakable carnage at any time and at any place.

Finally, the effects of technical sophistication were accelerated by the development of criminal groups from all points on the political-philosophical spectrum. These splinter groups have often joined forces through networks of computerized billboards and have been able to share information, resources, and personnel for matters of mutual concern (Mullins, 1997). What is particularly disturbing for law enforcement has been the realization that irrespective of their philosophies and ultimate goals, some of these groups share the commonalities of impressive armories of military weapons, the sophisticated training necessary to employ them, a proclivity for violence, and a total commitment to their causes. These factors have sometimes resulted in

undeserved and counterproductive media attention and the development of a sympathetic, if not enthusiastic, following that produces substantial financial resources. Unfortunately, the multifaceted composition of the American populace suggests that even more such groups
will develop. The willingness to employ deadly force against their perceived "oppressors" or against law enforcement officers or against
innocent bystanders, and the ability to do so is exemplified to some
degree or other by incidents described later in this book.

A CHANGE IN PROCEDURES: THREE EXAMPLES OF
NEEDED REORGANIZATION

Various large-scale and extraordinarily violent criminal events during the decade of the 1960s illustrated how traditional police methods
were inadequate and required the law enforcement establishment to
reevaluate its approaches when responding to such nonroutine calls
for service. The need for creating special tactical units to deal with special situations such as a barricaded suspect or a hostage seizure was
actually recognized after a series of unrelated incidents not normally
associated with today's SWAT teams.

For example, a rash of bank robberies in Philadelphia in 1964
resulted in the creation of a task force to apprehend very well-armed,
highly motivated, and apparently fearless criminals. The usual manner
of patrol officers answering a bank alarm after the perpetrators had
committed their activity seemed to be fruitless. Often outmanned and
usually outgunned, conventional responding officers were typically
too late to effect any sort of meaningful countermeasures. By focusing
on high-risk targets and responding as coordinated teams who were
trained, highly disciplined, and properly equipped, the task force was
able to lower the rate of bank robberies dramatically (Dempsey, 1994).
By definition, a task force is designed to address a specific problem
and then return to normal activity. So effective was this particular task
force that it has been retained as a permanent division of the
Philadelphia Police Department.

The Watts Riots in Los Angeles, California, began as a routine traffic stop on August 11, 1965. For reasons still unexplained with any
degree of unanimity, a simple arrest for drunken driving escalated into

a frenzy of anarchy, violence, and destruction. When it was over five days later, 34 persons had been killed and 1032 had been treated for injuries. The cost in property damage was beyond an accurate estimate.

The response of the Los Angeles Police Department was to "bring in more (police) cars." This approach was inefficient and, in many ways, a factor contributing to the problem. Since the cars came from different parts of the city, radio equipment was not calibrated properly to communicate with the personnel normally assigned to the area. As additional officers arrived, they found themselves without clear chains of command. Their confused appearance and failure to act as a coordinated unit did not promote effective operations nor did it enhance their image to the public.

Because the citizens' activities did not fall into normal definitions of riotous behavior, the responding officers were not prepared and lacked precise policies to follow. Officers were placed into assignments more on the basis of immediate availability and less for reasons of training, aptitude, or skill. Throughout the entire incident, the field commanders were improvising the tactics employed as the sequence of events unfolded, often resulting in unexpected consequences.

The department had usually been considered on the cutting edge of law enforcement technology. Now it found itself borrowing equipment from neighboring police agencies and allowing police personnel to purchase and use their own equipment. In many cases the diverse sources of equipment, particularly in communications, resulted in mass incompatibility and a severe handicap in information dissemination.

From a management perspective, the Watts Riots and the response by the Los Angeles Police Department revealed that the traditional approach depleted the ranks of the patrol force to such a degree that routine calls for police service were ignored. The departmentwide mobilization of personnel and the diversion of resources to the problems associated with the riot in Watts prevented responses to routine calls for service (Gates, 1992).

Depletion of the patrol force to deal with a special situation was again exemplified dramatically one year later halfway across the country in Austin, Texas (Mijares, 1993). The Texas Tower is a dominant feature of the Austin skyline overlooking the Main Building and the rest of the University of Texas campus. It has been that educational institution's landmark since 1937 and currently houses several administrative offices.

August 1, 1966, began as another day in the usually slow pace of a summer session at the university. By early afternoon, the campus would be covered with the blood of sixteen dead and thirty-two wounded victims of a demented sniper.

At approximately 11:30 a.m., a twenty-four-year-old student of architecture from Lake Worth, Florida, later identified as Charles Joseph Whitman, drove to an entry gate and requested a loading zone permit for a delivery at the Experimental Science Building. Whitman, a former Marine, did not go to his announced destination but proceeded to the Main Building. Upon arrival, he unloaded a footlocker from his car, placed it on a wheeled dolly and moved it to the 27th floor of the Tower using an elevator. He was seen by many people during the time he was transporting the footlocker from the street to the elevator, but he received no more than a casual glance since it was very common for delivery men to follow the same route. At this time in its history, visitors to the Tower could take the elevator to the 27th floor, pass a receptionist and climb three flights of stairs to the observation deck.[3]

Whitman removed his footlocker from the elevator and carried it to the narrow stairway leading to the observation deck. Sometime during this brief period he removed a shotgun from the footlocker, beat the receptionist to death with the butt of the weapon and shot four visitors who were approaching the observation deck on the stairs.

After barricading the stairway entrance with the dead receptionist's heavy desk, he carried the footlocker to the observation deck and removed a .30 caliber M1 carbine, a shotgun, a six millimeter rifle, food, water, and extra clothing. He placed the rifles and ammunition around the observation deck so that he could move from one position to another and continue firing without delay.

At 11:50 a.m., Whitman began firing at unsuspecting human targets on the campus below. At 11:51 a.m., an operator at the Austin Police Department's switchboard received a telephone call from Michael Hill of the University of Texas History Department. Hill reported that at least one person had been shot on the plaza immediately outside the Main Building. By the time Hill had given the operator the necessary information, over forty people lay dead or wounded at the scene.

---

3. After a student intentionally jumped to his death from the observation deck on October 28, 1974, the deck was closed to the public. It was reopened twenty-five years later with greatly improved security measures.

All available on-duty personnel from the Austin Police Department were dispatched to the scene with instructions to seal the area to pedestrian and vehicular traffic. Billy Speed, the first officer to the scene, approached from the south side of the Tower and was fatally wounded by Whitman's gunfire.

Local ambulance companies were dispatched to retrieve the wounded. Calls asking for additional personnel were made to the Travis County Sheriff's Office and the Texas Department of Public Safety. Requests were made to nearby military bases for armored vehicles to remove casualties from the streets. When none were immediately available, a local armored car service volunteered the use of its vehicles and drivers. Even funeral hearses were used to convey the dead and wounded to Brackenridge Hospital.

Because of the distance involved, normal police handguns were ineffective. Detectives were dispatched to the scene to provide suppressive fire. Many off-duty officers voluntarily returned to duty after hearing about the incident from news flashes on local radio and television stations. Other off-duty officers who had not heard the news were recalled to duty.

Much of the extra assistance was added to the Police Department's Communications Section. Telephone lines to the department were jammed with incoming calls from the public and the news media. Except for incidents involving violence or injury, no other routine calls for service were answered during the time when shots were being fired and casualties were being evacuated.

This general time frame was a period when police departments were reaping one of the benefits of the National Aerospace Administration's space exploration program by equipping their officers with portable radios. Unfortunately, these radios were in their infancy and were of limited transmission and reception range and battery duration. Because of a limited quantity, not every police officer was provided with this equipment. The officers who actually made their way to the inside of the Tower found that their radios were useless inside the concrete walls and they were forced to use telephones for communication purposes. The command post could serve as little more than a staging and briefing area. Consequently, coordinated arrest and rescue efforts and the maintenance of a span of control over the whole situation was impossible.

It has been suspected, but unsubstantiated, that well-meaning, but overzealous citizens of questionable judgment had armed themselves with hunting rifles and were taking shots at the sniper from several points around the Tower. It has been conjectured that some of the bursts near the sniper's position were not actually smoke from gunfire but were puffs of dust rising from the impact of the bullets upon the masonry from shots fired at ground level. Whether this suspicion about the source of these shots has a basis in fact is irrelevant. The fact that the possibility exists should be a cause for concern by the police manager because of risks to innocent bystanders and responding police personnel from unnecessary and preventable gunfire.[4]

A local pilot volunteered himself and his plane for observation purposes. The pilot and a police observer furnished information that there was only one man on the Tower. When the plane received two rifle bullets through the fuselage, the pilot and observer were ordered to withdraw.

At 1:00 p.m., a squad of officers was dispatched from the University Security Office with the objective of removing the wounded from the stairwell of the Tower's 27th floor. Since surface approaches to the Tower would expose them to direct shots from overhead, the group was led through a series of underground utility service tunnels that crisscross the campus. After entering the Tower from the tunnel system, they met another group of officers who had been able to approach from the sniper's rear.

Getting to the 27th floor was relatively easy. An upward approach to Whitman's position two stories higher on the observation deck offered a new challenge. Officers Houston McCoy and Ramiro Martinez, accompanied by civilian Allen "Cookie" Crum, found a scuttle hole that led to a ladder extending to a service area for the Tower's clocks. By climbing through a trap door on the ceiling of the service area, the officers found themselves on a roof above the observation deck. From this position Officer Martinez was able to neutralize Whitman with a shotgun blast, thus ending the rampage.

Considering the then-current state of law enforcement technology, the Austin Police Department and the entire community reacted very well to keep carnage from becoming unspeakably worse. Given the lack of an immediate response capability by law enforcement on col-

---

4. A similar set of circumstances took place in New Orleans in 1972. Suspect Mark Essex was killed approximately twelve hours after he had barricaded himself on the roof of the Howard Johnson's Motel. Yet, shots from the perimeter continued for twenty-five hours. These shots are believed to be from citizens and unauthorized police officers from outside the jurisdiction who had responded to the situation.

lege campuses and the absence of a precedent of this magnitude, the results are even more remarkable. The incident was characterized by individual acts of heroism and a spirit of collective, but unorganized, volunteerism under fire.

Because of his previous military training, Whitman was able to remove many of the tactical advantages normally sought by police officers responding to barricaded gunman situations. His selection of the highest available point allowed fields of fire not open to other barricaded gunmen. His line of sight rendered irrelevant the usual concepts of cover and concealment. By virtue of his isolation, any attempt to use a diversion would have been futile. These tactical considerations were factors over which the Austin Police Department had little or no control.

CONCLUSIONS

Administrative shortcomings in American law enforcement have sometimes become painfully obvious when put into the perspective of the type and magnitude of the events involved. These events have held separate but interwoven ramifications for the conduct of future law enforcement operations. First, they demonstrated that law enforcement technology was not yet sufficient to deal with many current problems. No longer was military surplus equipment adequate or appropriate for domestic applications. The Texas Tower incident in particular established an awareness of the need for a more sophisticated approach to communications.

Second, these incidents also led to an awareness of the need for firm, effective crowd and traffic control. Even under the most cordial and harmonious of circumstances, security is not a matter to be taken lightly. Entry of unauthorized personnel into an area of hostility not only impedes the conclusion of the incident and raises serious safety issues, but also can raise questions about liability for failing to protect noninvolved persons. In addition, confidence is raised when citizens see their police taking positive steps to isolate the risks to the public. For example, during the North Hollywood Bank Robbery in 1997 (see Chapter Five) responding officers brought resolution to a potentially catastrophic situation without injury to bystanders or substantial property damage. Considering how numerous people could have wandered into the field of fire in the commercial and residential areas involved, a major factor in the successful resolution of the incident may be attributed to the fact that the responding officers were able to isolate the perpetrators and that they made considerable efforts to block traffic from the area.

Third, these events illustrated how the complexion of many types of crimes was changing. The availability of large-capacity firearms and the sometimes direct involvement of a great number of people, both as perpetrators and as victims, were examples of how criminal activity was evolving and how law enforcement was forced to modify its approaches appropriately.

Alterations in criminal activity could be seen not only by the changes in participants and their technology but also by changes in overall strategies and specific tactics employed by the perpetrators. For the first time in the modern history of American law enforcement, responding police forces were confronted with perpetrators who were actually willing to die for a cause.

Where news coverage of these events had previously been limited to next-day reporting and analysis, technical advances in the news and entertainment media provided immediate telecast capability. Terrorist groups, though clearly guilty of criminal activities, achieved martyrdom among some segments of society. Not only were the perpetrators provided with a forum for their causes, critics of law enforcement were given a means to record and scrutinize the substance of what had occurred and how the police forces responded to the incident.

Finally, these incidents pointed to the need for law enforcement specialists who are trained to plan for and deal with unusual events as a coordinated unit without depleting the law enforcement agency's personnel or ability to respond to routine calls for police service. Special circumstances require specialized preparation in terms of personnel, technology, training, and tactics. No longer could any law enforcement agency assume that every member is prepared or equipped to perform any task on an *ad hoc* basis in response to this sort of increasingly complex and heinous criminal activity.

This need has proved to be particularly true in large metropolitan areas where multiple calls for this type of police service have become commonplace. Specialized preparation revolves around an organization whereby all functions associated with these perplexing problems can be performed in an orderly fashion without disruption to the other elements of the overall law enforcement agency. The term *organization* implies more than a recognized position in an organizational chart. The term carries with it the implication that any specialized component possesses the appropriate authority and means to perform any tasks for which it is responsible and that it receives the necessary support to perform these tasks.

Chapter Two

ORGANIZATIONAL ISSUES

The factual scenario which follows is derived from the trial court record in *Downs v. United States* (1975) as reported in the written opinion of the Sixth United States Circuit Court of Appeals. Also included is additional commentary by the Sixth Circuit as handed down in the case. The case provides a backdrop for discussions of organizational issues relative to the field of critical incident management. It likewise exposes the specter of civil liability risks. Because *Downs* contains facts that are also relevant to other areas, such as the planning and tactics of specific forms of incidents, it will be discussed here in some detail, and it will be revisited later.

In the early hours of October 4, 1971, the Special Agent in Charge of the Jacksonville, Florida, office of the Federal Bureau of Investigation was alerted about the hijacking of a private airplane in Nashville, Tennessee. The plane was reportedly headed for the Jacksonville International Airport and scheduled for arrival at approximately 5:00 a.m. Prior to departing from his residence for the airport, the agent in charge instructed his office to gather other agents thought to possess the skills necessary to deal with the situation.

Arriving at the airport shortly before the plane landed, the agent in charge received additional reports from his office that indicated that two armed men had commandeered the aircraft and had dragged a woman aboard while doing so. The woman was believed to be the estranged wife of one of the suspects. He also learned that the pilot of the plane had radioed the Jacksonville flight control tower and requested fuel, equipment to restart the engines, and other items, including maps and flotation gear for a flight to Freeport, Bahamas.

Additional agents arrived to join the agent in charge. These agents were eventually positioned in such a way that one was located in the

16

control tower to communicate by radio with the aircraft, and others were stationed approximately 200 yards from the hangar where the aircraft was to arrive. These agents were initially directed to hold their positions. A communications network was established whereby the agent in charge could use a two-way radio to speak with another agent in the FBI office. This agent could in turn communicate by telephone with the agent in the flight control tower. However, the agent in charge had no direct link to the tower and, therefore, could not directly monitor exchanges between the tower and the hijacked aircraft.

After the plane landed in Jacksonville, the agent in charge refused to allow refueling despite the pilot's report that the hijacker was in possession of an explosive device and posed a serious threat. The hijacker allowed the co-pilot, and later an armed associate to depart from the aircraft in order to negotiate for fuel. According to the trial record, the interviews conducted by the FBI agents with these individuals were abbreviated in nature and failed to solicit further information descriptive of the hijacker's mental state.

Despite the pilot's intonements that fuel be provided and that the agents stay away from the plane, moments after the hijacker's associate was taken into custody, the agents employed rifle fire to disable one of the plane's engines and attempted unsuccessfully to deflate the aircraft's tires. The attack provoked the hijacker to shoot and kill his wife, pilot Brenton Q. Downs, and himself. Pilot Downs's survivors sued the United States under the Federal Tort Claims Act[1], alleging that the FBI agent in charge had been negligent in handling the situation, a position with which the Sixth Circuit Court ultimately concurred.

Although the *Downs* opinion should not necessarily be read as providing a mandate to any police agency to organize a specialized tactical unit, it bears a message to the effect that once an agency in fact assumes responsibility for the resolution of extraordinary events, an *ad hoc* approach to management is highly undesirable. If the responsibility for such incidents is assumed with even the slightest of recurring levels of frequency, the agency can anticipate increased levels of

---

1. The Federal Tort Claims Act constitutes a broad waiver of sovereign immunity by the United States and gives federal courts jurisdiction to hear actions for injury or loss of property, for personal injury or death caused by the negligence or wrongful act or omission of any employee of the United States government while acting within the scope of employment. The liability laws applicable to the place where the act or omission occurred (typically those of the state of occurrence) are to be utilized. See generally 28 United States Code, Section 1346 (b).

scrutiny and accountability for outcomes as well. In short, heightened standards of the industry for the agency and the personnel who choose to enter into these situations will quickly come into play.

In the *Downs* example, the fact that the FBI had undertaken an organizational response to recurring situations involving aircraft hijackings appeared indicated by the existence of formal agency guidelines for dealing with them. But, are guidelines alone sufficient? Does an agency need the further capability of having at least some specialized officers who possess both particular experience and specialized training in applying those guidelines? The *Downs* court by implication suggested this may be the case by first observing that alleged errors on the part of a law enforcement agency are to be reviewed in light of the experience and training that officers may have or be expected to have in coping with the types of danger customarily assumed by agency members. Accordingly, the court concluded that the agents in *Downs* were to be held to higher standards of foresight into "better suited alternatives for protecting the hostages." Generally concurring legal support for this position is found in other references [*Restatement of Torts, Second*, Section 289 (a)(b)].

The *Downs* decision is by no means unique when read as saying that the more responsibility for others one attempts to undertake through experience, education, and the creation of organizational quality control mechanisms, the more one is placed at risk. Merely ask members of the medical profession about the distinction in liability drawn between those who are seen as professional health care providers versus simply good Samaritans. The question for police management and other government officials alike can quickly become one of "do we dare venture outward?" Though it requires courage to do so, to withdraw may be an abdication of both legal and moral responsibilities in view of the dramatic changes in American criminality, which were discussed in Chapter One. What follows hereafter are some organizational questions, observations and suggestions for consideration by police managers relative to the initial decision to create a true tactical response capability within the agency. These thoughts are presented along three fronts: First, what sort of organizational changes are necessary or desirable to establish and integrate an effective tactical capability within the existing structure? Second, how can the creation and maintenance of such capability be accomplished without placing prohibitive constraints on the agency's budget, personnel and other resources? Third, what fundamental civil litigation concepts should guide management planning?

IDENTIFYING ORGANIZATIONAL NEEDS AND GOALS

It is self-evident that not every critical incident rises to the incredible levels of risk to human life displayed during the Texas Tower Incident or the Watts Riot. Experience shows that the likelihood for such massive life taking or property loss are greater where large populations are concentrated in relatively small geographical areas, in short, in an urban environment. And yet, even in small cities or rural settings the occasions presenting circumstances beyond the traditional, routine calls for police services would seem to be on the increase. Therefore, police managers must attempt to recognize what are potentially the most likely nonroutine events their agencies will encounter given the dynamics of each particular community. And certainly special attention must be directed toward recognition of more hazardous situations that appear to be in transition from aberration into a new norm for the community.

An example of the "new norm" phenomenon may exist in the modern-day drug raid, a highly dangerous police function that no longer has exclusivity to large urban areas. A new capability to deal with this type of mission has become a necessary objective of many police agencies during the last two decades. Whether this capability is realized entirely within the local agency itself, or by resort to cooperative efforts with other agencies, care must be taken to avoid either the reality or even the appearance of carrying out an operation on an *ad hoc* basis. A case that may serve as an illustration is that of *City of Winter Haven v. Allen* (1989 and 1991) in which the surviving wife of a county deputy sheriff brought a wrongful death suit against the municipality on behalf of her husband's estate.

In the first of two trips through the Florida court system, the estate recovered a judgment in the amount of $600,000. The written opinion of the Florida District Court of Appeals following the first trial of the case discloses that in May of 1986, Polk County Sheriff's deputies obtained a narcotics search warrant for one particular room of a boarding house in the city of Winter Haven. It appears from this opinion that the Sheriff's Department was unable at the time to fill out a complete raid team, and, therefore, a request was made of the Winter Haven Police Department to provide "one or more of its officers to come to the briefing to be held before the drug raid that evening." The city responded by providing two officers who attended this planning session. At this meeting the raid team was advised that persons other than the suspects could be in the boarding house and that there was knowledge that the suspects might be armed. Although an order of entry into the house was established during this meeting, sheriff's deputies (including the decedent) eventually entered the front of the boarding house without waiting to verify by radio that the city police officers were in their preplanned positions at the rear of the structure.

The opinion next describes a seemingly chaotic set of circumstances in which at least two suspects, multiple deputies, and the city officers became involved. Subsequent to the frontal entry by the deputies, one suspect is described as taking flight down an interior hallway. Thereafter, another suspect is said to have waved a long stick at the decedent deputy and at least five gunshots fired were attributed to this deputy, all of which came prior to the city officers' arrival at the rear of the house.

Upon their eventual entry into the house, the city officers encountered another deputy dodging and weaving down the hallway in their direction. Believing this deputy to be under attack from some suspect, the police officers forced the deputy to the floor and "returned fire" by means of a single shotgun blast aimed back down the hallway toward a muzzle flash at the front of the house. Although contradictory evidence was heard, it was this shot that was identified as inflicting the fatal wound upon the officer. Ultimately, in the subsequent relitigation of the episode, a jury determined that both the deceased deputy and the city police officer firing the fatal shot were to some extent negligent under the circumstances.

While neither of the two appellate opinions disclose the previous history, if any, of cooperative drug efforts between the two particular law enforcement agencies involved, the opinions at least offer certain suggestions when read together. They point out that certain types of missions by their very nature epitomize both physical and legal perils possibly associated with improvisation of a single tactical assignment. Any mission with the implication for the use of deadly force by either suspects or officers must be approached as a highly coordinated team effort with appropriate attention to the composition of the team membership in terms of joint and multiple training opportunities and related strategies and techniques of execution. These common denominators for success should be implemented regardless of the individual identities of the team members and whether they are drawn wholly from within one agency or from multiple agencies.

Cohesiveness is an imperative that goes far beyond a superficial display of cooperative effort, however, and the truly effective tactical team must possess a strong sense of common purpose. This imperative will require the presence of structure. Therefore, the following concepts of structure are discussed along with suggestions for avoiding prohibitive pressures or constraints on agency budgets, personnel, and other resources in the implementation of a tactical unit.

ORGANIZATIONAL POLICY AND PROCEDURES

A *policy* is a clearly worded statement defining the actions to be taken by an organization and the reasons for that action. The statement should include the action, purpose, and the rationale for that purpose (Stojkovic, Kalinich, and Klofas, 1998). Policy serves as the linking mechanism between organizational goals and organizational procedures (Starling, 1998). Policy statements define lines of authority within the organization and subdivide the tasks (procedures) that must be followed in a specific sequence in order to achieve the goal stated in the policy.

A formal defined policy statement not only provides parameters for organizational methods, it also provides guidelines for individuals within the organization. Although a policy statement is usually a written document and published throughout the agency, unwritten or customary practices and *de facto* procedures may also become policy. More will be said later about the formation of informal norms and their potential impact on civil liability in particular.

An absence of behavioral limits for the organization's members is analogous to operating a watercraft without using appropriate oceanographic charts. Even with the best of intentions the helmsman who operates without the guidance of charts can endanger other crew members, destroy the ship, and become a navigational hazard to other marine vessels. Similarly, a specialized police unit that is charged with the responsibility of bringing the most violent of criminals to justice but which operates without carefully articulated policy can jeopardize the safety of the unit (crew) members, compromise the mission, and subject the organization to avoidable criticism and litigation.

Whether the situation involves a cruise ship on an ocean or a SWAT team in a metropolis, some sort of guidance is necessary to safeguard the organization and the individuals comprising it. The policy statement, when carefully planned and clearly articulated, offers the guidance needed to achieve organizational goals through operational procedures. A policy statement designed to link the organizational goals and operational procedures of a tactical unit should address such issues as the lines of authority, the chain of command, selection and training of personnel, media relations, command post operations, interactions with outside agencies, and general procedures to be followed by responding personnel.

Of necessity policy must be developed in accordance with relevant court decisions and legislation, social and political concerns, and budgetary constraints. Thus, developing a single policy statement that precisely fits the needs of all law enforcement agencies is of questionable merit and applicability. However, the International Association of Chiefs of Police, under United States Department of Justice Grant #87-SN-CX-K077, has developed "A Model Policy for Hostage/Barricaded Subject Incidents." With this policy comes the admonition that each police department operates in its own unique environment and that modifications of the model must be made accordingly.

INTRAORGANIZATIONAL PLACEMENT

One of the determinants of success among the world's elite counterterrorist units focuses on the location of these units within their respective organizations. Units such as Germany's GSG-9 and Great Britain's Special Air Service have been successful because their places on the organizational charts are directly under the organization's chief executive officer (Thompson, 1988). Such an arrangement promotes faster and clearer communications between the unit and the appropriate political leaders and expedites mobilization when necessary. The first-line supervisors of these units were responsible for making the tactical decisions during GSG-9's successful resolution of the Mogadishu Incident in 1977 and the SAS's notable achievement during the Iranian Embassy Siege in 1980. However, the timing of these decisions was largely dependent on negotiations and subterfuge operations conducted at the executive level. A complex chain of command would have unnecessarily complicated the issue and retarded these critical communications considerably. This sort of structure encourages a measure of participation by the agency leadership and promotes the executive support needed to turn stressful and often frustrating assignments within a bureaucracy into successful operations (Fyfe et al., 1997). Equally important, this sort of structure also prevents the development of rogue units. When elite units are distant from the chief executive in the agency's organizational chart, there is too much potential for unauthorized activities and unchecked actions. Even during the complete absence of any sort of impropriety, a misperception among the public and among the remainder of the organization can develop.

ORGANIZATIONAL COMMITMENT

Most large police departments serving a population of more than one million citizens with at least 1000 officers can easily justify the development and maintenance of a full-time tactical response unit. These units usually range from 20 to 150 officers. Because of the relative infrequency of traditional tactical deployments, personnel assigned to these units may also find themselves executing warrants, conducting training exercises, providing dignitary protection, carrying out search and rescue operations, and participating in myriad other law enforcement activities that require teamwork for effectiveness and release from routine assignments for organizational efficiency.

Although many of these activities take place without advance notice, most police departments cannot justify a full-time tactical operation on a twenty-four-hour basis from a cost-benefit perspective. Thus, even many large police departments are forced to be flexible in personnel scheduling and may require off-duty personnel to be subject to recall for a tactical deployment during normally low crime periods.

Medium-sized departments serving a population ranging from 50,000 to one million citizens usually find it more practical to maintain a part-time tactical operation. In this format each member of the tactical unit has a primary function within the overall organization and is mobilized into a structured, cohesive SWAT unit when necessary. Upon completion of these temporary duties, the officers return to their normal assignments. These officers may also be subject to recall during off-duty hours and normally are allotted tactical monthly training time on a regular basis.

Small towns, usually found on the fringes of a metroplex or in rural areas, generally do not receive calls for unusual circumstances in sufficient numbers to warrant a full-time or even a part-time commitment to establishing a specialized response capability. With some exceptions, most requests for police service in small law enforcement agencies can be categorized as "routine." Nonetheless, small town police departments report that the possibilities for some sort of extraordinary event always exist. Since budgets in these areas are usually stretched to the limit, the chief executives of these agencies find it difficult to justify expenditures on items that are unlikely to be used with any degree of certainty or frequency.

A fairly recent development in this area has been the development and utilization of *mutual aid pacts.* Under this concept small neighboring municipalities with somewhat limited resources have established formal agreements with each other to share personnel, equipment, and other resources on specific matters when it is not feasible for each municipality to provide the service alone. These services can include such diverse fields as narcotic interdiction, vice crime enforcement, communications services, organized crime control, hostage negotiations, DWI enforcement, and tactical operations.

The sharing of staff, tools, and other assets can take two distinct forms. *Task force* operations involve the allocation of equipment and transfer of personnel from each participating agency to a command structure that is separate from the participating agencies. Often the chief executive officer from each participating agency serves as a member of a board of governors which delegates authority to a task force commander. Depending on the size of the operation, the task force may be assembled initially for organizational familiarization and training purposes and later on a part-time, as-needed basis, with personnel returning to their parent commands upon completion of a specific task, or it may be a full-time assignment for both personnel and resources.

Direct assistance operations are more simplistic in their approach and do not involve a personnel transfer of any sort. Instead, an agreement is reached among participants before an emergency exists to provide each other with assistance only for the duration of the crisis. Upon conclusion of the emergency situation, all personnel and physical assets are returned to their parent commands. An extreme example of this concept was seen immediately subsequent to the tragic events of February 28, 1993 in Waco, Texas, when SWAT teams from cities throughout Texas rushed to the scene to assist local and federal officers after four agents from the Bureau of Alcohol, Tobacco, and Firearms had been killed in the line of duty. After the local officers had been properly relieved by federal agents, they returned to their respective parent commands to resume normal duties.

Irrespective of the type of mutual assistance operation being employed, police executives must answer several basic questions: First, what sort of legal authority exists in support of an interagency mutual assistance pact? Some states have enacted specific legislation to provide the guidelines for such affairs. For example, the State of Texas has devoted a brief section to law enforcement mutual assistance pacts in its Local Government Code. Under this statute the legislature acknowledged that many police agencies throughout the state are occasionally understaffed and underequipped and in need of assistance. Interagency cooperation for criminal investigation and law enforcement on matters of common concern is recognized as a valid tool in the criminal justice process. Both the "task force" and "direct assistance" type of arrangements are addressed in this statute (Perkins and Mijares, 1996). Police executives in other states would be well advised to confer with the department's legal counsel to identify appropriate authorizing state legislation before participating in any reciprocal relief agreement.

Second, what arrest powers are legally available to allow execution of the pact? Caution should always be practiced whenever officers from one jurisdiction engage in any law enforcement activities outside their official bailiwicks. Each state has some sort of statewide law enforcement training council, suggesting that every officer is charged with enforcing every state law in any part of the state. However, accusations concerning illegal arrest, improper searches and seizures, and unlawful use of force are persistent possibilities and should be specifically addressed during the contract formulation phase of any mutual assistance pact.

A somewhat simplistic approach is to cross-deputize every assigned officer each time the task force or direct assistance operation is utilized. This practice may be, at one extreme, unnecessarily redundant or, at the other extreme, an area where an inadvertent omission could lead to questionable legal authority. A preferred method of resolving the ambiguity is through the wording of the enabling statute to assert that while an officer who is regularly employed in one jurisdiction is assigned to the task force, all law enforcement powers of any participating agency are retained.

Third, on whom will the responsibilities for managing the agreement ultimately fall? Signatories to the agreement should define the specific supervisor/subordinate relationship, identify the specific chain of command, and acknowledge the source and formulators of operational policy long before the creation and use of the task force. A common practice is to designate the heads of all participating agencies as a board of governors for the regional task force. The board is responsible for selecting a task force commander, establishing selection criteria, determining training standards, and formulating operational policies and procedures (Perkins and Mijares, 1996).

Fourth, what administrative issues should be covered in the formalization of such a pact? These issues include responsibility for overtime compensation, payments for medical expenses incurred through work-related injuries, compensation for court appearances resulting from enforcement action taken while deployed to the task force, and any other expenses associated with the compensation of personnel of any bureaucratic organization. Just as water seeks its own level, these expenses can be expected to be equalized among the participating agencies in the long run. Thus, the signatories to a mutual assistance pact must agree in advance that either the requesting police agency absorb all the expenses of a given incident or the supplying police agency could pay only the expenses incurred by its own personnel during the incident. Regardless of the option exercised, the details could and should be negotiated in advance and agreement on financial responsibilities should be reached before the contract becomes officially operational. To operate without a contract identifying these financial obligations could leave the individual officer uncompensated and unprotected in the event of a disabling injury.

Finally, how is the concept of civil liability affected by participation in a mutual assistance pact? What vicarious responsibilities may loom?

CIVIL LIABILITY AWARENESS

While police managers should not be expected to display the same levels of expertise in civil litigation as lawyers who are routinely engaged as plaintiffs' attorneys or defense counsel, some basic familiarity with civil tort actions can be of great benefit. If nothing else, a grasp of cornerstone theories of police liability and possible defenses to liability will enable police administrators to recognize more accurately when they are "getting in over their heads." Police administrators provide their officers, their agencies, and the elected officials who employ them a great service by keeping abreast of evolving legal precedents in police liability. One must candidly be able to assess one's own levels of awareness and understanding of these precedents and know when to seek the professional assistance of experts in litigation in the formation and implementation of policy.

Beyond the preventative medicine approach to policy management, police officers of all types and particularly at the management level, including immediate supervisors, should understand that a working knowledge of legal fundamentals will greatly aid the communication between the police and any attorneys called upon actually to defend against the civil claim. In short, the "defense team" composed of the police client and lawyer will necessarily become stronger if there exists even a basic, common denominator and reference point of legal understanding. This common ground routinely exists between police and prosecuting attorneys in the realm of criminal law cases. The proliferation of civil litigation aimed at police demands a similar approach toward defense of the police.

Finally, the police manager must recognize a further duty that is owed by the law enforcement agency directly to the employing governmental entity and indirectly to the general public. The reality is that the government entity rather than individual police officers is normally the preferred target of civil litigation. Seeking the "deeper pockets" of the government to satisfy any monetary judgments awarded, plaintiffs have a variety of legally approved theories with which to connect the government to the misconduct of its police forces. Some of the more fundamental and commonly employed theories will be discussed here shortly. To the extent that plaintiffs are successful in these connective efforts, it is ultimately the taxpaying public that bears the financial burden of actual judgments against "their government." Even successful defense against such claims can be quite costly in terms of legal fees and court expenses. Therefore, the primary management goal returns as always to formulating the most effective total package for keeping the tactical unit at a level of competence that will discourage all but the most obviously frivolous lawsuits. There will always be some of that form of litigation beyond the control of the police.

Litigation Cornerstones

In general, causes of action against the police come in three categories. They consist of common law tort actions, statutory tort actions, or constitutional tort actions. A cause of action is a reason for bringing a lawsuit before a court seeking judicial relief that is recognized in the law. A tort is a wrong or injury done to a person (called the *plaintiff*) in violation of a duty imposed by law upon another person (called the *defendant*). The duty breached does not arise from a specific agreement or contract between the parties, but rather from the factual connections that exist between the plaintiff and the defendant. Therefore, every tort action requires the existence of three elements. These elements are: (1) some duty from the defendant to the plaintiff that under the facts of the case is recognized within the law; (2) a failure to fulfill that duty by the defendant; and (3) damage to the plaintiff as a result (Black, 1979). For example, the police owe a duty recognized by law not to use excessive force in arresting a person. This duty is not created by any contract that exists between an arresting officer and the person arrested. It is a duty that the law of torts, rather than the law of contracts, has recognized. If the police breach this duty and cause harm, then the law of torts recognizes a remedy for compensation of the person arrested.

Common Law Tort Actions

The common law must be distinguished first from law that is created exclusively by legislative action in the form of statutes. American common law is really a body of legal theories and principles that originated and developed in England centuries ago. Figuratively speaking, the English common law crossed the Atlantic Ocean during the American colonial period and was subsequently adopted in most of the states. It is based upon concepts of causes of action protecting both personal and property interests which by custom have been protected by most societies since time immemorial (Black, pp. 250–251). These protective customs, though unwritten, were recognized and enforced by early English courts. Much of modern law takes the form of written statutes, but tort law remains largely unwritten in the sense that it is not set out in statutes or codes. However, it can be found written in a different sense on a case-by-case basis within the recorded judgments and opinions of the various appellate courts in this country (Prosser and Keeton, 1984). Indeed, it is within these written opinions that tort litigation attorneys commonly practice their trade, and more pertinently, where police administrators with the assistance of counsel must remain abreast of prior case scenarios that have given rise to lawsuits against law enforcement personnel.

Usually, though not always, tort liability is predicated on the concept of "fault." This approach is a moral concept which in turn recognizes various degrees of blameworthiness (Prosser and Keeton, pp. 21–23). Police officers can perhaps identify with this concept by remembering analogous concepts within the criminal law. For example, the definitions of most crimes set out various elements. Commonly these elements include the performance of some act coupled with the existence of a particular state of mind which then results in some harm to a victim. Also, some criminal statutes state that the "act" element of the crime is in reality "a failure to act" where the law places some duty on the person to "behave" in a way that does not produce harm. But, regardless of whether the prohibited behavior is an act or a failure to act, the criminal law normally requires that a culpable (or blameworthy) mental state coexist. Thus, both criminal law and tort law usually place significant emphasis on moral fault as evidenced by the defendant's state of mind. In the criminal law context the Model Penal Code recognizes four such states of mind by degree of blameworthiness. From highest degree to lowest degree these states are: (1) purposely, also known as intentionally; (2) knowingly; (3) recklessly; and (4) criminally negligent. The level of punishment for a crime is commonly directly related to these varying degrees of blameworthiness.

Likewise, the common law of torts has recognized various degrees of fault that must be proved in order to sustain a particular form of tort action, and to differentiate levels of monetary damages accordingly. As one will see, these states of mind are often somewhat interchangeable with recognized criminal states of mind. Also, depending upon the various jurisdictions, both criminal statutes and tort law have sometimes used other words to describe different degrees of fault. This reality often has led to great confusion, as if any attempt to put any mental state into words was not already difficult enough. Thus, commonly used mental states within the law of torts have come to include intentional, willful, wanton, reckless, gross negligence, and negligence. While precise definitions have proved elusive, generalizations may be offered.

If one acts "intentionally," it is probably with the specific purpose or objective of causing harm. "Willfully," "wantonly," and "recklessly" are very much akin to one another in terms of degree of fault. With none of these states of mind is specific intent to do harm present. Rather, conduct occurs under circumstances in which the actor knew or had reason to know that his or her behavior created a very great risk of harm to others. Put in other words, the actor is (or is presumed to be) conscious of the risks involved, but is indifferent or callous in his or her disregard of the potentially harmful consequences (Kionka, 1992).

Yet another literary term for a mental state that lies in the same gray vicinity as that of willful, wanton, or reckless has also emerged within the courts. This term is not frequently found used in the context of common law causes of action, but rather in cases involving the other two previously mentioned general categories of litigation called statutory and constitutional torts. This term is deliberate indifference and more will be said on this topic later. It is introduced now simply for relative comparison with the other degrees of fault under discussion.

"Gross negligence," though not as blameworthy as any of the above-described mental states, is nonetheless still a significant degree of fault. This state of mind denotes not conscious creation of risks, but rather their unconscious creation. Although no actual awareness of risk creation is involved, the failure of the actor to recognize the risk factors at work and behave accordingly is deemed under the circumstances to be a gross or very substantial deviation from what the average person would have perceived or actually recognized and done.

Finally, when a person acts "negligently," there is simply either a failure to perceive risk or to behave in a manner that the ordinary, reasonable, and prudent person would have done. While this failure of perception and behavior is not as dramatic as with gross negligence, it is nonetheless sufficient in law to ascribe fault to the defendant. Another significant point should be made here about assessment of when and under what circumstances an actor is negligent. Where an actor has elected to participate in functions that require expertise acquired through specialized education, training and/or experience, then the actor will be held to a higher standard of conduct than that of the ordinary person. This higher standard of conduct includes not only a greater recognition of potential risks associated with a particular set of factual circumstances, but also greater care or skill utilized in dealing with the situation. In general, these higher standards are commonly associated with the "professions." Medical practitioners, for example, are held accountable along these lines for allegations of malpractice (Abraham, 1997). Skilled tradesmen or other occupations in which licensing or certification is required denoting a person as a member of a more qualified group of specialists are other examples where this theory might come into play (Kionka, pp. 52–53). Even the novice member of the field is required to measure up to what has been repeatedly referred to in this work as the "standards of the industry."

In the context of tactical team management, supervisors must, therefore, understand that the novice individual officer or the novice tactical team collectively may be held to standards with which they are not yet prepared to comply. Therefore, an agency may be far wiser in neither creating nor deploying a SWAT team until the commitment to selection, training, equipping, and evaluating the team is commensurate with the higher accountability standards that may simultaneously arise. Even though one might argue that entry into the arena of SWAT operations has become necessary or at least socially useful for a particular community, the police administrator simply must not take on this added responsibility until the agency is properly prepared. Particularly to be avoided is the creation and deployment of a team based primarily on motivations of enhancing the public image of the agency or individual or agency morale. To create form over substance is in itself inherently indicative of negligence in the management function. It is also to invite litigation directed at supervisors and local government entities on the basis of vicarious civil liability.

Vicarious Liability

Vicarious liability is a form of liability by which one person or legal entity is held liable for a tort committed by another person, usually an employee (Kionka, p. 229). Typically, within the context of policing, this concept would involve a tort committed by an individual police officer during the course of employment which results in the officer's supervisors or employing governmental entity being sued along with the officer.

Numerous treatises assert that justifications for vicarious liability are grounded both in public policy and in practical realities in terms of achieving meaningful remedies for individual plaintiffs who have incurred harm. From a public policy perspective it may be appropriate that vicarious liability exists because it is often the supervisor/employer who is in control and orders the employee into a tort-generating contact with the public. It is also believed that vicarious liability will tend to serve the additional purpose of forcing supervisors and employers to formulate and implement policies that will reduce further incidents of harm causing behaviors by employees for the good of the entire public.

Practically speaking, in many instances it is only the employee's "superior" who possesses the financial resources to compensate a plaintiff adequately for the harm suffered. The individual employee such as a police officer or officers who directly caused the harm simply do not have the funds to accomplish the goal at hand. Indeed, individual supervisors likely have the same limitations, and therefore, the governmental entity must bear the burden. The losses sustained from injuries caused by employees are simply a cost of doing business that the employer can more easily absorb and pass along to the public or through insurance (Prosser and Keeton; Kionka; Harper, James, and Gray 1986; Speiser, Krause, and Gans, 1983).

Directly related to the imposition of vicarious liability under common law tort actions is the legal principle known as *respondeat superior*, meaning, "Let the superior answer" (Abraham, p. 182). Where the superior (employer) is in fact a governmental entity, common law tort actions have evolved to a state of recognition not only within the courts, but within legislative bodies as well. This evolution means that common law actions aimed at the government are now specifically provided for by statutes commonly known as tort claims acts. Such statutes exist at the federal level in the form of the Federal Tort Claims

Act[2] and in some form or other within virtually all states. Should one be inclined to inquire as to why legislative codification recognizing the validity of such claims came into being, the answer to that question has at least two facets.

First, one historic legal rule was that governments could not be sued for the torts committed by their employees, including their police officials. This rule, called "sovereign immunity" first existed in English custom and law. It employed, among other rationales, the logic that "the king could do no wrong." (Of course the king did not exactly want to share his wealth with subjects harmed by his servants, either!) Obviously sovereign immunity of this traditional sort does not fit neatly within the constitutional republic form of government established in this country. However, the protection of the sovereign's assets continued to have vitality as a policy recognized in American jurisprudence (Kionka, p. 342). For while the specific identity of the sovereign may have changed in this country from monarch to federal and state governmental entities, the need to immunize those sovereignties in the interest of maintaining their financial solvency lived on. Today, however, for the sake of balancing the sovereign's interest with that of the individual citizen who has been harmed by government employees, sovereign immunity has been waived to various degrees by the tort claims acts previously mentioned. While recognizing the right to sue the government for at least some forms of torts committed by its employees exists, these acts normally place limits or caps on the total amount of monetary damages the government must pay.

Secondly, another significant requirement of these statutes which remains to protect the government is that the tort must have been committed by an employee while acting within the scope of employment (Abraham, p. 183). Scope of employment issues have sometimes been hotly debated in the courts in individual cases. Other exceptions to these statutes' applicability, such as the so-called "discretionary functions" exception, commonly exist in a legislative attempt to retain some further remnants of sovereign immunity (Prosser and Keeton, p. 1039). A complete analysis of these various exceptions can often become quite esoteric and lies far beyond the scope of this work. Indeed, achieving consistency and precision in rulings on the applicability of tort claims legislation has proved perplexing to the courts themselves.

---

2. The Federal Tort Claims Act constitutes a broad waiver of sovereign immunity by the United States and gives federal courts jurisdiction to hear actions for injury or loss of property, or personal injury or death caused by the negligence or wrongful act or omission of any employee of the United States government while acting within the scope of employment. The liability laws applicable to the place where the act or omission occurred (typically those of the state of occurrence) are to be utilized. See generally 28 United States Code, Section 1346 (b).

A final point worthy of mention here is that tort claims acts should not be confused with "statutory torts" which will be discussed in the next sections. Tort claims acts do not create new causes of action against the government so much as recognize by statutory formality the right of a citizen to pursue, subject to expressed limitations, the older common law tort actions.

Statutory Torts

In addition to common law actions against individual officers or officials and suits brought against government entities under tort claims acts, there exist other supplemental forms of tort actions with implications for the police. Several federal statutes have been passed by Congress to protect the rights of individuals under the United States Constitution and its Bill of Rights. One of these statutes also provides additional remedies for violations of other individual rights that are secured not by the Constitution but rather through other federal statutes.

The Congressional act referred to is 42 United States Code, Section 1983, a federal statute that most police administrators have by now grown accustomed to hearing about. Since its early origin this statute has been referred to as the "Ku Klux Klan Act" arising as it did out of the reconstruction era following the American Civil War. Passed at least in part to deal with actual or perceived violations of rights of citizens at the hands of state and local governmental officials, including law enforcement officers, in the aftermath of the war, the statute has experienced a monumental rebirth in recent years. It reads:

> Every person, who under color of any statute, ordinance, regulation, custom or usage, of any State or Territory, subjects or causes to be subjected, any citizen of the United States or any person within the jurisdiction thereof, the deprivation of any rights, privileges, or immunities secured by the Constitution and laws, shall be liable to the party injured in an action at law, suit in equity, or other proper proceeding for redress.

By its own wording and through interpretation of its language and Congressional legislative intent primarily by the United States Supreme Court, the following general legal principles have emerged relative to this statute:

1. Any individual state or local governmental official, including a police officer, who violates any civil rights of another person while acting within the scope of that official's employment may be the subject of a lawsuit filed either in the federal or state court systems of the jurisdiction wherein the alleged violation occurred. The rights referred to include not only those protected by the United States Constitution but also any other civil rights created by federal statutes. Therefore, Section 1983 actions may be extremely wide in scope. Within the context of police functions, illegal arrests, searches and seizures, unnecessary and excessive use of force during arrests, intentional assaults and wrongful deaths all immediately come to mind as common but not exclusive sources of litigation under Section 1983 (Kionka, p. 297).

2. Local governmental entities such as municipalities and counties can under certain circumstances be joined as defendants along with individual governmental officials (police officers and their supervisors). The United States Supreme Court has ruled that these local governments are also "persons" within the usage of the term "every person" in the beginning language of the act. However, liability can only be imposed upon the local governments where harm is found to have been caused as a result of an "official policy" of the governmental entity (*Monell v. Department of Social Services,* 1978). Considerably more will be said of what factors go into assessment of the term official policy in a later chapter. For now, it should suffice to say by oversimplification that official policy can arise directly as a result of statements, written or verbal, from high-ranking officers or indirectly through time-honored informal customs or norms of practice. The significance of this official policy requirement is that Section 1983 actions are available only when harm-causing acts by local government employees can fairly said to be "the acts of the government itself" rather than the personal misbehavior of individual officers. Vicarious civil liability through application of the doctrine of *respondeat superior* to employing governmental entities is not present in Section 1983 cases. In short, a local government has no liability exposure solely because one of its employees has violated a plaintiff's rights while on the job. This difference from tort claims acts cases is distinctive and crucial.

3. Potential plaintiffs include all "persons," whether they are citizens of this country or other persons within the jurisdiction of the United States (Harper, James, and Gray, p. 736). (Consider briefly the conceivable implications of this principle in the context of a tactical episode involving foreign terrorists or foreign hostages.)

4. Unlike claims brought under tort claims acts, there are no limits or caps on the amount of monetary damages that plaintiffs can be awarded. This rule together with another federal statutory rule allowing for separate and complete recovery of attorneys' fees for prevailing parties has no doubt contributed to the immense popularity of Section 1983 actions among plaintiffs and their lawyers (Harper, James, and Gray, p. 743).

5. As to the issue of "fault" or "culpable mental state" needed to be proved for a successful outcome for the Section 1983 plaintiff, unfortunately the existing case law is fraught with inconsistencies and contradictions. Section 1983 itself contains no identified mental state within its language. Therefore, the courts have been left to struggle between both Congressional legislative intent (if any even existed in 1871) and traditional common law tort principles regarding mental states (refer to prior discussion of common law fault herein). Apparently, no specific intent to violate a plaintiff's civil rights must be proved, though clearly such an intent would be sufficient to satisfy any requirement of fault. As far as actions against individual officers are concerned, depending upon the court studied, the range of fault specified as sufficient for recovery of damages has been described in a confused body of cases which include the entire mental state continuum from intentional down to negligence (Mijares and Perkins, 1994). However, the key case of *City of Canton v. Harris* (1989) identifies "deliberate indifference" toward civil rights on the part of city policy makers as the mental state needed to subject a municipality to Section 1983 liability. Recall here that deliberate indifference is akin to recklessness in the disregard of risk to others. This case is worthy of considerable attention and is discussed at some length in Chapter Four as it pertains to the training needed for tactical assignments.

Constitutional Torts

In enacting Section 1983 Congress provided remedies against persons acting under color of state law. However, the statute does not address violations of civil rights at the hands of federal officials or employees. It must be recognized that the same types of constitutional harms can be committed by agents of the federal government as by those of the states. In an effort to fill this void and to provide fuller protection of civil rights, it has been held by the United States Supreme Court that a parallel form of action can be maintained against federal officers directly under the Constitution even though no separate statute similar to Section 1983 exists as to the activities of these officers (*Bivens v. Six Unknown Agents of the United States Bureau of Narcotics,* 1971).

In bringing this preliminary overview of tort principles to a conclusion, it would be remiss to leave the impression that because there are several, if not numerous, tort theories that plaintiffs may conceivably pursue, plaintiffs are routinely successful in their lawsuits against the police. This stance would of course completely ignore the reality of both factual and legal defenses that the law of torts also recognizes. Once again it should, therefore, be noted that a full and complete exploration of the multitude of such defensive concepts as contributory and comparative negligence, defense of self or others, assumption of risk, necessity of action, authority of law, actions taken in good faith," qualified or absolute immunities, etc., is the stuff of which an entirely separate and voluminous legal treatise could be formed. In any specific case any one or more of the above defensive theories (or others not mentioned herein) may apply depending in turn upon the plaintiff's specific choice of tort action and the underlying law of the applicable state or federal jurisdiction involved.

It is the authors' belief that in the final analysis, it is more important for police officials to have a working knowledge of the theories behind the various potential tort claims that plaintiffs may bring than intricate awareness of defenses. This opinion is due to the fact that defenses are for the most part "reactive" mechanisms to offset civil liability. In oversimplified terms, defenses tend to either exist or not exist in retrospective analysis of liability cases. Good defense counsel can usually identify arguable defenses after the fact. But, it is a poor police officer and certainly a poor police manager who relies primarily upon the potential existence of a legal defense to guide police behavior and certainly the formulation by management of overall police policies. The existence of defenses should be viewed more as last resorts to avoidance of judgments after police activity has occurred, and not as primary factors in police policy and planning operations. On the other hand, developing a prior understanding of the bases for various forms of tort actions is forward looking in nature and a proactive approach by management. Therefore, it tends to far better serve both the police and the public through application of the axiom that an ounce of prevention is worth more than a pound of cure.

Chapter Three

THE SELECTION OF TACTICAL OFFICERS

Once the decision to implement a tactical team has been made, the personnel selection process assumes the utmost importance. Following a brief description of earlier methods of selecting personnel for tactical assignment, various principles of public personnel administration will be discussed with particular references to the demands of tactical operations and current judicial review of relevant issues. Finally, a consensus model of selection will be proposed. This model is based on an integration of the present personnel administration practices discussed in the text and the resources currently available to tactical units throughout the United States.

EARLY METHODS OF SELECTING SPECIALIZED PERSONNEL

Because of the accurate perception of the need for teamwork, the earliest selection methods were often based on the "Good Old Boy" network.[1] If a candidate was not compatible with the already assigned personnel, he was disqualified from further consideration for assignment. Acceptability was based on extremely arbitrary criteria such as social favoritism and political considerations. Without valid criteria for assignment, an otherwise qualified candidate could be denied assignment to the tactical unit.

In some instances a candidate was selected for assignment because he owned a necessary piece of equipment such as a high-powered rifle

---

1. When tactical teams were initially made operational during the late 1960s and early 1970s, female officers were a novelty even in general patrol functions. The idea that a female officer would ask for consideration for assigment to a tactical unit was not an issue for discussion at that point in time.

with a telescopic sight. In these cases, it was assumed that the individual also possessed the necessary skills to use the equipment effectively. The question of physical or psychological fitness for the assignment rarely, if ever, became an issue.

Previous work records were also given consideration as criteria for selection. A rough assessment could be made of the candidate's motivation to excel and of his quantity and quality of productivity by an examination of measurable data such as the number of felony and misdemeanor arrests made, the number of tickets written, the amount of court appearances, the conviction rate, the frequency of sick-time usage, and the number and disposition of citizen complaints made against an officer.

RELEVANT ISSUES OF PUBLIC PERSONNEL ADMINISTRATION

Classification for any occupational position, whether it is in the private sector or in public service, is based on a variety of factors. A further perspective into the methods for identifying and selecting personnel for specialized police assignments can be obtained through an analysis of seven different classification factors (Fine, 1974). Fine's established principles of personnel management can then be examined in light of the particular demands of a specific assignment to a police tactical unit.

Fine's question of **Information Input** asks where and how does the employee receive the information used in performing the job. Essentially, the evaluator is asking how trainable is the applicant for the job. Records of work-related training, both at the recruit and advanced levels, will provide a substantive indication of the applicant's previous training. When these records are compared to specific items in the individual's personnel file, the reviewer can gain an insight into how well the individual has put this training into operation.

For example, an officer who has attended regularly scheduled driver education programs yet continues to have numerous on-duty traffic accidents is experiencing difficulty absorbing theory and data and applying them to the demands of the work environment. The tactical officer will be expected to undergo a level of training that far exceeds the level attained in basic training at the recruit academy. (See Chapters Four and Five for specific information regarding training.) The officer's ability to apply this training to the solution of dangerous and critical problems will directly affect the performance and safety of his fellow officers and innocent victims as well as himself. Like many other factors of job classification, this element can be examined through a review of the candidate's previous work record.

Fine also defined the concept of **Mental Processes** which seeks to know what reasoning, planning, decision-making and information-processing activities are involved in performing the job. The tasks of a tactical officer must be performed rationally. Any obstacles to job completion must be overcome without compounding the problem with undue displays of emotional frustration. Clinically this ability can be examined through various standardized psychological tests and interviews. Practically it can be observed by a review of previous work records, conversations with current coworkers and supervisors and by interviews with the candidate. Further observations can be made by observing the candidate's decision-making performance during simulation exercises and hypothetical situations.

The concern with **Work Output** asks what physical activities does the employee perform and what tools or devices does he or she use? Tactical operations often require a great deal of strenuous activities that involve physical fitness. Physical fitness has also been associated with mental ability and emotional stability in numerous studies and can be measured through several testing procedures (Cooper, 1977). An increased capacity for work, more efficiently achieved production levels, and decreased absenteeism are also strongly correlated with physical fitness. These positive attributes are behavioral characteristics desired in any employee.

Since many police departments do not require or provide a physical conditioning program for their officers, requiring a specific level of physical fitness serves as an indirect measure of initiative, self-motivation and self-discipline. The same level of physical fitness can also serve as a requirement for continued assignment long after initial selection to the tactical unit.[2]

The issue of a candidate's **Relationships with Others** addresses what social relationships are required in performing the job. Because

---

2. Informal interviews with several tactical unit supervisors suggest that the overwhelming majority of incumbent officers far exceed physical fitness requirements on a regular basis.

of the extremely close interdependency required among officers in training and in actual operations, tactical officers must put aside personal differences and biases not only for the maintenance of group integrity and proper mission completion but also for personal survival.

Many of the social skills needed by a tactical officer can be developed primarily through experience as a police officer. A minimum of three years is usually considered to be necessary not only to learn these skills but also to learn and understand the officer's own abilities and limitations. Relationships with citizens, coworkers, supervisors, and other officials of the criminal justice system must be cultivated with time and exposure. Consequently, the criterion of time on the job and previous assignment becomes critical. Assignments in staff positions may be a personal preference and an organizational necessity, but these assignments do not contribute meaningfully to the potential tactical officer's relevant work experiences.

The **Job Context** defines in what physical and social context the job is performed. The tactical officer operates in a wide variety of physical and social settings. Physical endurance and mental patience are characteristics desired in any police officer. The tactical officer must possess these characteristics in their highest form and must display them in each operation.

During the evaluation of the initial group for training in the Detroit Police Department's Special Response Team, the examining officers found that participation in team sports and certain military assignments are excellent means for developing the personal skills that are needed to mold a group of individuals into a cohesive unit. The tough-talking "loner" homicide detective depicted as "Dirty Harry" may be an interesting fictional character. However, without the sense of team effort, he would not be an effective tactical officer.

The category of **Work Methods** asks what methods or techniques are used to perform the job. In many job classifications this factor often involves a task analysis for a complete description of the methods for assignment completion. Since the actual tactics vary considerably from place to place and from one time period to another, a generic approach to methods may be meaningless. However, there can be agreement that the overall goal of a tactical unit is to contain, control, and de-escalate a critical situation.

One of the best indicators of future behavior is past behavior. An examination of the officer's reports on previous incidents, interviews with supervisors and coworkers and conversations with the candidate can give an indication of his or her tendencies to attain this goal in previous assignments and operations.

Fine's final issue of **Worker Traits** describes what personality characteristics or aptitudes are needed for satisfactory job performance. Various authors have developed extremely broad behavioral and experiential characteristics desired in tactical personnel. Each of the authors possesses a wealth of experience and offers a solidly based normative profile. Kolman (1982) stresses emotional stability, flexibility, and maturity in tactical personnel.

Jacobs (1983) advocates a tactical officer with above-average intelligence with a desire to expand his or her knowledge. The officer should possess emotional stability and should react appropriately under stress. In particular, the officer should not be argumentative at the scene of an incident.

Through the use of a variety of psychological testing instruments, several characteristics were found in candidates for assignment in the Special Enforcement Detail of the San Diego, California Sheriff's Department (Cole, 1988). These characteristics include the following:

1. Slightly higher-than-average levels of intellectual capacity, decisiveness, self-reliance, and assertiveness
2. Strong heterosexuality
3. Variations in activity, people, and surroundings
4. Detached, formal, and aloof interpersonal relationships
5. Concern about how others regard them

To gain an understanding of the current practices for selecting tactical personnel, MacKenna and Stevens (1989) surveyed 456 police departments in cities with a population of 50,000 or more. Forty-one percent of the departments responded to the survey. Of these, 90 percent indicated that a tactical unit was operational within the department. The results of the survey indicated that while commanding officers of these units rated psychological factors as the most important considerations for selection, current practices continue to favor physical fitness, seniority, and firearms proficiency as prime determinants. Each of these practices merits attention.

First, physical fitness is directly related to many of the activities performed by the tactical officer. An officer assigned to SWAT may be expected to run, jump, climb, or crawl just to attain an operational position. The officer may then be expected to remain motionless for long periods without relief before engaging in various forms of the martial arts. The officer may also be required to carry an injured victim or even a criminal to a place of safety for treatment. These activities are usually performed under great physical and psychological stress and without the luxury of an athlete's warmup period. In addition, several studies have shown high correlations between physical fitness and work-related behavioral characteristics, such as emotional stability, self-confidence, production, and job satisfaction (Price, Pollock, Gettman, and Kent, 1977). Consequently, physical fitness is one of the most commonly employed criteria for the selection of tactical officers.

Second, the role of seniority assumes more importance than following traditional practices or mere compliance with a collective bargaining agreement. Logic suggests that longevity tends to eliminate psychologically unfit officers from the organization. This form of personnel elimination is a naturally occurring phenomenon through a process of self-weeding. It is also an institutional phenomenon through established disciplinary and termination procedures. With maturity, a police officer becomes less impulsive and more cognizant of personal limitations. Such an officer takes less unnecessary risks and tends to be more diplomatic during conflict resolution.

Logic also suggests that seniority is related to job knowledge. Certainly the tactical officer must understand the substantive and procedural issues of law enforcement. The officer must also possess a firm grasp of the social and political context in which law enforcement operations are conducted. This knowledge includes an awareness of the objects of concern (victims as well as criminals) and it must include a sensitivity to coworkers. Time and experience allow the officer to develop and refine these necessary knowledge areas. They also allow the officer's supervisors and peers to obtain the data necessary for making informed decisions about the officer's request for assignment to the tactical unit.

Finally, firearms proficiency remains a criterion for the selection of tactical personnel despite the fact that it is a skill that can be developed through proper coaching from training officers. Often the strong emphasis on firearms proficiency is misinterpreted as a "macho" fixation or Freudian fascination. Nothing could be further from the truth. The emphasis is a direct function of the critical nature of the proper use of firearms placed on law enforcement personnel by the courts, politicians, and society in general. Because this particular aspect of any police officer's duties is considered to be the "final option" and the ultimate exercise of constitutional authority (Perkins and Mijares, 1997), the use of firearms is the single most serious and decisive responsibility performed by any American law enforcement officer. Consequently, much emphasis is necessarily attached to a reliable, appropriate and accurate use of firearms.

Questions about firearms proficiency extend beyond the measurement of how well a candidate can place little holes in a paper target from a selected distance. Management must also be concerned with how well the candidate adapts to levels of training and how progressively skills are improved. Firearms proficiency is one of the quantifiable skills where an officer's training progress can be measured and compared in a longitudinal assessment. A steadily rising score is an indicator of a candidate's ability to be trained and desire to improve.

Another aspect of firearms proficiency is equipment and its maintenance. Tactical personnel are entrusted with equipment that is far more sophisticated than equipment possessed by the general patrol force. This equipment includes advanced weaponry, communications devices, and surveillance apparatus. An insight into the candidate's ability to maintain and use the more technical equipment can be gained by observing the ability to maintain and use the department firearm of standard issue.

Finally, examination of an officer's use of weaponry can also give an indication of the officer's compliance with established firearms policies. A history of inappropriate discharges and unjustified allegations of excessive force may be grounds for disqualification from further consideration for selection.

SELECTION OF TACTICAL PERSONNEL AND CIVIL LIABILITY

The various considerations in the selection process noted above have ramifications for police supervisors beyond the obvious desire to maximize both individual officers and tactical unit effectiveness. Unfortunately, the issue of vicarious civil liability for both supervisor and employing government entity may again exist in the event of errors or omissions in selection and assignment decision making.

Negligent or otherwise misguided assignment of personnel to positions for which they are inadequate to respond competently due to either physical, intellectual, or emotional shortcomings has been the subject of claims by plaintiffs for monetary damages directed at police supervisors. Commonly, supervisors have defended against these lawsuits by asserting that while they may be responsible for having selected and assigned officers whose actions caused injury to others, as supervisors they bear no legal responsibility because they have not participated personally in the harmful behavior, nor have they either directed or condoned it. The issue, thus, becomes narrowly framed in terms of the supervisor's legal responsibility for simply having failed to act properly in the original screening and assignment task.

This issue can arise in any number of assignment-specific circumstances. These circumstances may include the negligent failure to transfer a patrol officer with a history of brutality complaints to a less-sensitive position with minimal public contact. They may also include the failure to recognize and avoid the selection of a tactical candidate who, by service record and valid testing, may be an inappropriate selection for assignment. In short, a failure to avoid the type of personality perhaps most likely to employ excessive force in the emotion-charged tactical environment may subject the law enforcement organization and its administration to avoidable criticism and possible litigation.

Supervisors may, therefore, be in legal jeopardy on at least two theories. First, that their selection and assignment of unqualified personnel was a direct personal act in and of itself bearing responsibility for the harm suffered by a plaintiff who has received excessive police force. Second, ironically, comes the theory of liability that a "failure to act" appropriately by imposing standards of officer competence necessary to ensure the reasonable safety of a plaintiff constitutes a breach of an affirmative duty with respect to the plaintiff, and that such failure to fulfill this duty was the cause of the injury. A representative case conjuring up both of these respective theories of liability related to police supervisors is found in *Moon v. Winfield* (1973 and 1974) as well as in other case authorities cited within that opinion. The case is therefore recommended as additional reading for the student of the legal relationship between failures to select tactical personnel properly and supervisory civil liability.

A RANGE OF APPROACHES TO THE SELECTION OF TACTICAL PERSONNEL

Law enforcement agencies throughout the world have developed several approaches for the selection of personnel to be assigned to a tactical operation. Insight into the various selection processes was obtained through on-site observations by the authors and through examinations of department manuals of procedure from several law enforcement agencies. Through these observations and through interviews with incumbent tactical officers, an operational perspective has been integrated with the existing literature, resulting in the development of the following general approach to selection. The following approach is actually a range of several different selection procedures and may justifiably be called an eclectic approach to personnel selection for tactical operations. Under the current guidelines established by the Equal Employment Opportunity Act of 1972, there can be no absolute standards or universal criteria in personnel management. Through self-analysis each employing agency must establish its own specific personnel needs and limitations as well as its own norms for satisfactory test performance.

One of the purposes of a **medical examination** as a selection tool is to allow the personnel manager to focus on those positions that have a high rate of on-the-job injuries, illnesses, or substance abuse (Klingner and Nalbandian, 1985). As indicated earlier, the position of tactical officer is one of the most physically vigorous job classifications in modern law enforcement. Consequently, the candidate for selection to a tactical team must be free from medical conditions that could become symptomatic disabilities as a result of performing these activities.

Because of the high expense associated with this phase as well as its undemonstrated utility, most departments do not employ a medical examination as a process in the selection of tactical personnel. As a representative of the highest level of the law enforcement agency, the modern police administrator is required to be sensitive to both its value and its cost.

The agencies that do employ a medical test rationalize the need on the basis that the position of tactical officer is one of the most physically vigorous job classifications in modern law enforcement. Here it is anticipated that the expenses for workers' compensation, medical treatment, and replacement personnel can far exceed the initial costs of a task-related medical examination. This approach takes the position that the candidate should satisfactorily pass the medical examination before further testing is conducted. The physical testing that follows and the later job demands of tactical assignment can both cause disabling injuries. Allowing a candidate to participate in these strenuous activities, both the preparatory testing and the eventual SWAT duties, can subject the administrator to allegations of negligence and liability subsequent to an injury.

The **physical testing** of candidates requires a minimum of staff, equipment, and labor. A review of the literature addressing physical fitness as a selection criterion indicates that the usual focus of attention has actually been directed toward entry-level selection, not toward selection for specialized assignments. The requirements are not expected to identify Olympic athletes but are intended solely to identify candidates who possess the basic muscular strength, agility, and cardiovascular endurance needed for satisfactory completion of training and assignment to the tactical unit. Of primary importance is the need to meet the objectives of training and assignment without injury.

The physical testing procedure is intentionally not skill-oriented. Testing for developed skills at this phase requires the candidate to have undergone earlier tactical training and eliminates officers who would otherwise be trained if given the opportunity.

The **three-mile run** is a typical measure of the candidate's aerobic capacity. It should be run non-stop on a flat, dry surface such as a quarter-mile running track at a local school. Ideally, the same weather conditions will exist each time the test is conducted. Training on a sloping road or wet field may be more realistic after being selected to the tactical team, but in the interest of consistency and safety during the selection process, it is more appropriate to run on a track.

It is much easier to monitor the status and physical condition of the runners when a track is used. It may also be anticipated that there will be candidates who have not prepared adequately for the testing despite any announcement of the requirements made in advance of the actual testing. With memories of high school athletic feats accomplished several years ago, these officers may have deluded themselves into believing that they have remained in good shape by playing in a softball game every week. Pulled muscles, sprained joints, and even cardiac arrests are very real possibilities when administering any sort of physical testing to middle-aged police officers. Consequently, it is prudent for the test administrator to announce the test criteria long in advance and to make arrangements for an ambulance or other form of emergency medical service to be available at the test site.

Administration is relatively easy. A group of candidates is gathered at a designated line on a track and given the command to start. As the start-finish line is crossed after each lap, each candidate gives his name and lap number to the scorer. This procedure not only assists the recording of the laps finished, but also provides an indication that the runner is conscious of all surroundings and personal condition.

Upon completion of the run the candidate is directed to perform satisfactorily in a series of exercises to assure that the upper body strength and muscular endurance needed to perform job-related tasks such as climbing, rappelling, hand-to-hand combat, and equipment movement are possessed. The whole issue of muscular strength and endurance is one of significant importance in the selection of tactical officers. A task analysis of any tactical unit would indicate that the assignment is one of the most physically demanding in modern law enforcement. Typically, a tactical officer must be able to run at top speed for 30 to 100 yards before scaling a vertical surface, often without the aid of climbing apparatus. The candidate for selection must be able to support his own body weight while engaged in various activities such as rappelling. The candidate must be able to carry a heavy battering ram from a parked vehicle to a barricaded scene and then immediately use it to force entry. The candidate will be required to employ a variety of martial arts to block, parry, counter and subdue an aggressive subject. The candidate must be able to carry an unconscious person to a place of safety. To compound the situation, these tasks are typically performed without the benefit of an athletic warmup in rapid succession and usually under great psychological stress. In most cases, the officer is carrying several pounds of equipment and wearing a 30-pound protective piece of body armor when performing these tasks.

Clearly, these tasks require considerable muscular strength and endurance. An officer who does not possess the physical ability to perform these tasks is not only unproductive but also is a distinct liability to the organization, a hazard to other unit members, and a risk for serious personal injury. However, the use of physical testing of candidates for any specialized position is not without some controversy and potential legal challenge. In general, women tend to possess less upper body strength than men. This tendency can evoke an apprehension that physical testing can discriminate against female applicants.

In response to an allegation of gender discrimination in its SWAT selection practices, the Los Angeles Police Department initiated an examination of its methods. This process first identified the frequency, intensity, and duration of ten general tasks performed during barricaded suspect operations and crisis negotiation activities. An analysis of these general tasks defined 32 specific rating factors or KSAs (knowledge areas, skills, and abilities) needed to perform these tasks with acceptable competence.

Seventeen different tests determined the competency level at which each applicant performed. During the testing the evaluation team was to be cognizant of the following factors in each candidate:

1. Psychological/emotional characteristics
2. Knowledge of police procedures and skills
3. Personal characteristics and attitude
4. Attention to detail
5. Reasoning and judgment
6. Oral communication skills
7. Interpersonal skills
8. Ability to learn and memorize
9. Medical condition

Candidates received one of four grades (outstanding, excellent, satisfactory, or unsatisfactory) for each of the seventeen tests and, based on their overall scores, were placed into a pool for further consideration. Ultimately the case was settled out-of-court on unrelated grounds. However, the testing process was recognized as valid and reasonable because of its direct relevance to the work environment.

Any department intending to develop a tactical unit or add personnel to an existing unit should announce the time, date, location, and requirements of physical testing well in advance. This procedure allows the candidate the opportunity to prepare for the testing. The tactical team training supervisor should be able to provide the physical training guidance for personnel who may be interested in the training but who may need some form of instruction about how to train to meet the standards. Finally, in an instance of failure to meet these standards, an opportunity to re-take the physical fitness test should be extended to any applicant who can otherwise meet the requirements of assignment to the tactical unit. Thus, the physical fitness test is not actually an elimination device but a means of motivating law enforcement personnel to develop and maintain a level of physical fitness that would allow them to participate safely and without compromise in the training and actual functions of tactical operations.

Several questions about the candidate remain unanswered by the medical examination, physical fitness test, and psychological evaluation. The administrator may also be concerned with issues such as the candidate's reaction to extreme provocation, the candidate's ability to complete the training and to apply the new skills to a tactical assignment, and the candidate's ability to become a group-oriented tactical officer after years of individuality as a patrol officer. Many of these questions about the candidate's future behavior can be best answered by examining past behavior. The **background investigation** provides the means for acquiring information about the candidate's past.

Much of the information needed can be found in the candidate's personnel file. Quantifiable data such as numbers of arrests made and traffic tickets written give an indication of the candidate's production orientation or job enthusiasm especially when compared to numbers of arrests and tickets generated by other officers in similar assignments. When these numbers are compared in terms of court cases and convictions, an indication of the quality of production can be developed. Officers whose comparative quantity and quality of production is higher than average tend to be the professionally aggressive type of officer sought in tactical personnel.

However, high quantity and quality production takes on a new meaning if they are accompanied by a high number of substantiated citizen complaints and internal discipline actions for violations of department rules and regulations. A professionally aggressive officer can expect to receive more complaints simply because of the greater frequency of interacting with criminal violators. In most cases, these complaints are unfounded and are actually a rationalization for criminal behavior (Sykes and Matza, 1957). However, if there is a trend for substantiated complaints, the candidate is likely to continue this behavior even after transfer to a specialized unit.

Another method of determining an individual's motivation to achieve can be found in the level of formal education and specialized training. Since many police departments still do not require a higher level of education beyond high school graduation, any higher education is done only through the initiative of the individual. This sort of motivation to achieve an education is a characteristic highly desired in any officer applying for a specialized position.

Tactical operations are team efforts. Each member's action directly affects the actions and safety of other officers. Since behavioral predictability is such an important factor in this specialized assignment, the background investigation must pay close attention to the candidate's attendance record. Police officers can be expected to be ill at some time of their careers. Exposure to contagious diseases, working in inclement weather and assignments with irregular hours can contribute to an officer's health problems. However, when an officer has been reporting sick with a pattern (e.g., in conjunction with a vacation or a regularly scheduled leave day), there is cause for the police administrator to be concerned. In many cases, the excessive use of sick-time is an indication of any of a variety of emotional and behavioral problems. From the normal supervisory perspective, this officer presents problems with employee scheduling and morale. The employee must be predictable in attendance in order to allow the organization to function properly. Assignment to a specialized unit generally will not improve an individual's poor attendance record or behavioral unpredictability. From the perspective of tactical supervision, this officer may not be present for all phases of training and would be a distinct liability during operations. As a result, a history of excessive sick-time usage should be considered a cause for rejection.

With some minor exceptions, police officers work as individuals. Each officer has great discretion about when and where to initiate contact with citizens, what sort of enforcement action will follow, or what sort of service will be rendered. Tactical operations are group operations. Each member of the group must function as part of a well-oiled machine. The safety of the group and its members and the success of the mission is dependent on the ability of each member to perform assigned tasks. Experience has shown that the attitudes and behaviors needed in tactical operations can be developed through participation in team sports and through military experience. This information is usually found in the recruiting section of a candidate's personnel file. Although a lack of experience in the military or in team sports need not be considered a cause for disqualification, candidates who have engaged in these activities will be operating at a distinct advantage and will be definite assets to the specialized unit.

The **personal interview** allows that candidate to demonstrate qualities that are not normally revealed through the previously mentioned selection tools. The traditional interview served two purposes. First, it served to verify or clarify information already developed through the background investigation. Second, the interview has been used as a primary method of rejecting candidates who may look good on paper but might not fit into an organizational unit (Schmitt and Coyle, 1976). Without definable and valid criteria on which to base the interview, the interview has been subject to close scrutiny as a selection method (Dipboye, Fromkin, and Wiback, 1975).

To be effective and defendable, an interview must be conducted with purpose and structure. The traditional interview often consisted of a supervisor or a team of supervisors who would simply ask the candidate why a transfer to the specialized unit has been requested. In many cases the most important criterion of the interview was the candidate's appearance. The candidate would appear in a new, freshly pressed uniform replete with highly polished leatherware, firearms qualification badges, meritorious service insignias and spit-shined shoes. Questions would be raised about any absenteeism, citizen complaints, or internal investigations. These questions usually required only a "Yes" or "No" response without specific details. In many cases the decision to accept or reject the candidate had already been made and the interview was merely a formality. In short, the traditional personal interview lacked definable objectives and consistency.

In response to criticism directed toward the personal interview, some employers have used the more comprehensive approach of the assessment center to evaluate candidates for employment, assignment, or promotion. In most instances the practice is directed toward middle and upper management positions (Byam and Wettengal, 1974). Since the candidate for selection to the tactical unit remains at the operational level, the entire assessment center may not be necessary as an administrative tool. A modification of this personnel selection technique can greatly assist the evaluation team in the identification of candidates for a tactical unit.

By employing a variation of the analytic problem of the assessment center, the evaluation team can meet several specific objectives which are relevant to the dynamic nature of tactical operations. First, the candidate can demonstrate the capacity to identify and retain salient information. Second, the candidate can display the ability to formulate a feasible plan of operation based on the available information. Third, the candidate can demonstrate the ability to communicate this plan to a group of simulated users of the information.

CONCLUSION

Law enforcement officers who are assigned to tactical duty must display many personal characteristics not normally addressed in most discussions of selection criteria. The need for these characteristics is the direct result of the practical, legal, and ethical considerations that must be made by the chief administrator. Failure to establish and abide by relevant and appropriate selection criteria not only compromises efforts to complete the mission of the tactical unit but also subjects the administrator to avoidable allegations of negligence.

Chapter Four

INITIAL TACTICAL TRAINING

PURPOSES OF TRAINING

The need for training in law enforcement has been recognized since the days of August Vollmer. This need was officially recognized by Congress in the passage of The Omnibus Crime Control and Safe Streets Act of 1968. Although much of the public attention to this Act was directed toward the underwriting of equipment for use by local law enforcement agencies, the bulk of the allocations were for the development of criminal justice personnel through training and education programs.

The need for training was also recognized by the states through the creation of state regulatory agencies whose specific mission was to define the curriculum content and to operationalize the process of law enforcement training. In most instances the primary training concern has been focused on entry-level recruits as the recipients of this training. However, after Congress refused to renew the terms of the Act in 1980, many states took it upon themselves to increase the frequency and variety of law enforcement training by mandating all current law enforcement personnel to complete a minimum number of training hours per year to maintain certification as a peace officer. Some states have even taken a further step by requiring law enforcement personnel to undergo regularly scheduled instruction, retraining, and testing to maintain specialized certifications for positions such as radar operators and intoxalyzer operators.

Training is much like art; i.e., most people have an idea of what it is, but few can define it, differentiate among its various forms or identify its purposes. Training is an essential and continuous process in the management of any law enforcement context. It is necessary for successful operations and must be carefully addressed in order to avoid entangling legal controversies.

Thus, the intention of this chapter is to define the purposes of law enforcement training in general, to suggest specific curriculum approaches for varying needs and budgetary constraints in the preparation of tactical personnel, and to identify different styles and sources of initial tactical training. Throughout the chapter attention is directed to the overriding legal issues which guide the development of any training program.

Training in any organization serves multiple purposes and, when conducted properly, achieves many goals (Bopp, 1974). First, the trainee learns the rules and regulations of the organization. While an officer who has been newly selected for tactical training may already be familiar with the general orders of the overall police department, the specific policies and procedures of the tactical unit must be learned. For example, the new tactical officer must become familiar with such procedures as personnel mobilization methods, duty schedules, equipment logistics and allocation, and other elements specifically relevant to the new assignment and its administration. The SWAT instructor must carry this purpose into training and reinforce the agency's policy on the use of firearms and force (*Wierstak v. Heffernan*, 1986).

The trainee must also learn the new skills and behaviors associated with the new assignment. *Canton v. Harris* (1989) strongly suggests in its admonition that specialized police personnel must receive training in the express tasks related to a particular job assignment in the police organization. For example, team movements and dynamic entry techniques are regular tasks performed by a tactical unit. To avoid legal controversy as well as operational failure, the new tactical officer must be instructed in all the tasks to be performed in this new assignment. The police culture in general is a learned culture. Just as a police cadet officer develops new attitudes and behaviors, the new tactical officer must develop and refine a new perspective on containing, controlling and de-escalating a situation through patience, persistence, and practice. For example, as a police officer advances from recruit training to the role of patrol officer, a certain level of self-reliance and a sense of independence are developed. Techniques are learned to increase levels of suspicion without paranoia, to become assertive without brutality, and to respond quickly without haste. A tactical officer learns to be patient without being complacent, to persevere with emotional detachment without becoming insensitive, and to function as a part of a well-oiled machine without feeling like a mere cog.

Initial tactical training provides the means to learn the techniques and technology of the new assignment. The law enforcement scientific revolution that has taken place since the mid 1960s has produced a gap between the development of technology and the ability to apply and use it. Through proper training this gap can be narrowed. For example, thermal imagery was originally developed for an industrial need to detect heat transfer and the resulting energy and structural fluctuations. When applied to a law enforcement context, thermal imagery can be used to locate suspects when vision is limited, to verify illegal narcotic processing operations, and even to find buried corpses through the heat generated from normal organic decomposition. Knowledge of and familiarity with this equipment may result in a safer way for tactical officers to approach barricaded suspects (Perkins and Mijares, 1998). Even the most sophisticated police officer cannot be expected to master the complexities of this technology without detailed training and practice.

In order for law enforcement personnel to utilize this equipment properly, they must be trained in its use and the users must also be allowed to practice their skills on a regular basis. For example, Michael Jordan possessed a great deal of innate athletic ability and was arguably the best basketball player ever to play the game. Yet, he continuously sought to improve his skill level under the watchful eye of his coach. Because of the critical nature of the tasks performed and the relative frequency for the employment of these extreme measures, tactical personnel must be similarly able to demonstrate their skills more frequently and under conditions of greater stress and examination than other law enforcement personnel. Once the new skills are learned, they must be demonstrated regularly with a semblance of reality under close scrutiny and demanding supervision. To apply a standard of less than excellence would be counterproductive and may subject the organization to avoidable criticism and possible litigation (Perkins and Mijares, 1997). Thus, training can also serve as a means to identify shortcomings in personnel and equipment through practice and constructive criticism.

CURRICULUM ISSUES

Most initial tactical training programs consist of an introduction to such topics as the history of specialized police operations, physical fitness, individual and team movement, entry techniques, chemical agents, less-lethal technology, hostage negotiations, building searches, precision marksmanship, and the effective neutralization of threats from barricaded suspects. These programs tend to consist of forty to sixty hours spread over four to six days. A typical basic curriculum is found in Table 4.1. While the development of individual knowledge, skills, and ability is important, the progression from a group of skilled individuals into a unified, coordinated team is heavily stressed.

Table 4.1
TACTICAL TRAINING PROGRAM BASIC CURRICULUM

Subject	Hours Required
Orientation	1
History	2
Equipment	1
Basic Operations	2
Case Studies	2
Physical Training	5
Rappelling	2
Team Movement	2
Sniper Operations	3
Less-lethal Technology	4
Entry Techniques	8
Night Operations	8
Hostage Negotiations	4
Raids	5
Confidence Course	2
Combat Pistol	3
Written and Practical Tests	4
Awards and Critique	2
TOTAL	60

Ideally, the training methods will follow a progressive desensitization process whereby the instructor breaks down each technique into its most basic parts. The component parts are taught one at a time in a series of graded exposures, cumulatively added together with gradually increasing degrees of difficulty and realism, and repeatedly practiced under the scrutiny of the instructor. However, with the severe time and budgetary constraints encountered by most police departments, the instructional methods usually are limited to an instructional block taught in the setting of a classroom demonstration followed by a very brief opportunity to perform the techniques. Programs of such short duration tend to be the norm and the only source of instruction for many tactical units throughout the United States.

At the opposite extreme of the continuum, the curriculum for the initial training of the Detroit Police Department's Special Response Team consisted of 640 hours. This program, which was previewed by the Michigan Law Enforcement Officer Training Council before actual implementation, was designed with three important considerations. First, the training was to be content valid whereby only the scenarios likely to be encountered within the Detroit jurisdictional boundaries would be included in the curriculum. Training in irrelevant techniques and technology was considered a waste of valuable time and a distraction from the important tasks at hand. Based on an instructional model used by West Germany's GSG-9, the trainees performed the newly learned skills under realistic simulations. It would make little sense to dress in jungle-style battle dress utility uniforms (BDUs) and practice long-distance cross-country navigation in an urban setting highly based on industry and commerce. Second, initial instruction would be provided by a training corps specifically versed in both tactical operations and teaching methods. During actual tactical missions the training corps would serve as intelligence analysts. When not involved in the tasks of training or intelligence analysis, the instructional staff would conduct research and tactical product evaluation. Finally, a collegial approach to further training, evaluation, and operations would be fostered once the initial training phase was completed. The trainees ultimately developed teaching skills as well as the basic skill levels needed for successful assignment in this new position. A summary of the curriculum is found in Table 4.2.

Table 4.2
TACTICAL TRAINING PROGRAM COMPREHENSIVE CURRICULUM

Subject	Hours Required
Introduction to SWAT Operations	2
Basics of Psychology and Sociology	2
History of Terrorism	8
Legal Issues of SWAT	8
Crisis Entry	58
Searches	36
Hostage Negotiation	50
Combat First Aid	4
Weapons	126
Physical Training	142
Bomb Scene Management	8
Surveillance Techniques	6
Intelligence Analysis	6
Dignitary Protection	8
Chemical Agents	6
Terrorist Weapons and Tactics	6
Dynamic Entry Techniques	12
Defensive Tactics	28
Rappelling	100
Protective Driving	6
Private Security	4
Testing	10
Program Critique	2
TOTAL	640

SOURCES OF INITIAL TACTICAL TRAINING

Officers selected for tactical assignments can obtain their initial tactical training from a variety of sources. The International Association of Chiefs of Police, the Federal Bureau of Investigation, the National Tactical Officers Association, and many state associations of tactical officers each provide several different relevant courses of study to develop and improve police performance levels. These sources are generally good foundations of information, but because of time limitations, do not allow a measurable amount of performance demonstration or evaluation. Because officers from several different police departments may be in the same class, these courses are normally taught in the most general of terms with only minor adjustments for variations brought on by factors such as budgets, size, and geography.

A second source of initial training can be found through existing SWAT teams. It has become fairly common for some of the larger police departments to include training slots for officers in smaller departments. Again, it is difficult to tailor a training program for the specific needs of these officers when using this approach.

Another source can be found among tactical equipment manufacturers and distributors. Most of these sources provide training only in the use of their specific products. A small number of weapons manufacturers, such as Heckler and Koch and Smith and Wesson provide an introduction to a wide range of tactical topics. Many of the instructors are former police officers with a great deal of practical experience. Like the initial approach of using established tactical training programs from the FBI, the IACP and the NTOA, this training strategy offers a wide range of resources such as management and legal advice to accompany the practical issues.

A final source of training comes from entrepreneurial sources. Often staffed by highly skilled retired military and police personnel, these training companies provide excellent means of developing tactical abilities. However, the application of these abilities must be conducted within the parameters established by relevant court decisions, existing legislation, and current departmental policies. In some instances these companies are staffed by foreign personnel who have operated in an entirely different law enforcement context and environment. It is the responsibility of management to ensure that these parameters are included in any instruction related to the use of force (*Wierstak v. Heffernan*, 1986). Possession of these necessary skills by the instructional staff without the actual police experience in their appropriate application is not only meaningless but can lead to errors in judgment by the trainees, which can detract from the fulfillment of the organizational mission.

All of these approaches involve considerable expense in terms of travel and lodging. For all but the largest police departments, developing an entire SWAT unit using either of these methods can be cost prohibitive and a practical impossibility in terms of the release time needed to accomplish the task of training.

A combination of these approaches was followed by the Detroit Police Department. The Tactical Mobile Unit (TMU) had been created under a federal grant in 1965 to serve as the department's strike force for a variety of unusual circumstances such as crowd control, barricaded suspects, dignitary protection, and many other activities requiring a large police response without depleting the ranks of the patrol force. As the first unit in the department equipped with car-to-car and portable radios, the unit performed saturation patrol in high crime areas when not engaged in the specific duties of its original mission. Later named the Tactical Services Section (TSS) in 1974, the unit grew to its maximum size of 120 officers in the 5000-member department and took on additional duties such as dignitary escort service, K-9 patrol, warrant service for the investigative units, and patrol support for understaffed precincts.

In 1984, Detroit's mayor, Coleman A. Young, became alarmed by a wave of international terrorism. After he professed his concern that the department's tactical response capability was in need of modernization, a small cadre of training officers was identified from the existing ranks of the department for an additional tactical unit, the Special Response Team, which became part of the Tactical Services Section. All of the training officers had earlier served as instructors at some time during their careers and were selected on the basis of their research capabilities, experience in the field of tactical operations, and expected ability to guide the concept of a SWAT team into an operational reality.

The training cadre visited equipment manufacturers and other law enforcement agencies, such as the Los Angeles SWAT team, Great Britain's Special Air Service (SAS), and West Germany's Federal Border Guard Group Nine (GSG-9). They also visited specific sites throughout the Detroit area. Based on information gathered from these sources, the training cadre developed operational procedures, personnel selection criteria, and the instructional materials. This approach to training has since been used by many police departments to train specialized personnel in a multitude of assignments (Treusch, 1991).

TRAINING SITES

Many of the basic tactical skills can be learned in a typical police academy environment. A classroom equipped with a speaker's lectern, student seating, chalkboard, overhead projector, a video cassette recorder (VCR) and monitor, provides the fundamental facilities needed to conduct the lecture portion of the training. This portion of the instruction can be enhanced by using a computerized multimedia approach, such as Power Point to involve as many of the human senses as actively possible.

A gymnasium equipped with shock-absorbing mats and protective equipment is necessary to learn and practice the necessary take-down and restraint techniques. Ideally the gymnasium will also contain progressive resistance equipment, either free-weights or machine, and cardiovascular facilities and apparatus such as a running track or treadmill, stationary cycles, and rowing machines to build and maintain anaerobic and aerobic capacities.

A firearms range is needed to become familiar with all weapons in the SWAT armory. These weapons include handguns, shotguns, assault rifles, sniper rifles, less-lethal devices, and chemical agent dispersal tools. A wide variety of firearms ranges exists throughout the world of tactical operations. Some tactical units have simply used an abandoned rock quarry as a firearms range while at the other end of the spectrum, Germany's GSG-9 has been provided with several indoor and outdoor ranges complete with bulletabsorbing tile and moveable walls for varying scenarios. In one section of the complex the trainees can practice on the fuselage of a jetliner in the event of another Mogadishu Incident. Tire houses, paintball ranges, and simmunition training provide variation and application between these extremes on a cost effective basis.

Some tactical units have found rappelling to be a relevant skill and have constructed rappel towers for this purpose. Other units have installed whole villages of potential tactical scenarios. Several law enforcement agencies have become very creative in the construction of their training facilities. Inmates (Los Angeles County Sheriff) and military assistance (Abilene) have often been used to provide labor while civic groups and police vendors have provided raw materials for the project.

THE RELATIONSHIP OF TRAINING TO
CIVIL LIABILITY ISSUES

Appropriate levels of training can significantly reduce the potential for successful litigation against individual officers, supervisors, and, indeed, the governmental entities by whom tactical personnel are employed. This observation is not to say litigation will be forestalled completely simply by intensifying training efforts, but it may serve to discourage it substantially in individual cases.

Causes of action against police are most commonly thought to arise within the context of claims leveled by civilians alleging the use excessive of force. Plaintiffs bringing such actions to bear may include both criminal perpetrators and innocent bystanders to an incident in which force is utilized. However, on some occasions within the context of alleged inadequate training, the plaintiff might even be a fellow officer who becomes a casualty of misapplied "friendly fire" attributable to other officers.

Allegations of negligence in training tactical officers properly so as to minimize the risk to all varieties of players involved may arise under the tort laws of the individual states. The currently most popular form of civil action, the federal Section 1983 lawsuit, expands the scope of potential liability beyond individual officers and police supervisors to include local government entities such as cities and counties. This expansion may occur when malfeasance in the training function is especially acute in light of the usual and recurring duties assigned to particular officers and thus becomes a "policy of inadequate training."

The seminal case on standards for imposing Section 1983 on local governments for failure to train is now generally recognized to be *City of Canton v. Harris* (1989). Although on its facts *Harris* is not a use of force case, it has been cited as binding authority in a large number of subsequent force specific cases arising within the nation's lower courts. The range of the use of force cases applying *Harris* standards for training currently runs a gamut from the activities of common patrol officers to an analysis of training adequacy in a tactical unit situation (*Alexander v. City and County of San Francisco*, 1994).

In *Harris* the United States Supreme Court ruled on whether local municipality liability in a Section 1983 suit may be predicated on the inadequate training of police officers responsible for the medical needs of detainees prior to admission to the city jail facility. The City of Canton had provided a written policy in a general fashion for routine first aid training for its shift supervisors and to authorize their referrals of detainees to medical professionals for more specialized treatment. In April of 1978, Mrs. Harris was arrested and brought to the local police station in a patrol wagon. Upon arrival at the station, she was found sitting on the floor of the police vehicle. Asked if she needed medical attention, she replied incoherently. During the subsequent processing she fell to the floor twice. Officers left her lying on the floor and no medical attention was ever summoned. She later claimed that the training of shift commanders was inadequate in her case insofar as recognition of the severity of her symptoms. She alleged that the resultant failure to summon proper professional medical assistance in a timely fashion under the circumstances was a violation of her due process rights. Thus, even though the city had a policy directed toward the protection of prisoners who were ill, the question was whether a lack of proper training resulted in the unconstitutional application of that policy in her case. Testimony in the case did indeed suggest that Canton shift commanders had not been provided with any special training as to when to summon medical professionals.

Writing for a majority of the Court, Justice Byron White observed that this central issue in turn became whether the city's policy was adequate in light of the duties assigned to certain individual officers and that the focus must be on the adequacy of that policy in relation to the tasks that those *particular* officers must perform considering the *usual* and *recurring* situations with which they must deal. An often-quoted footnote of the opinion[1] recognizes that even in certain forms of routine police activity the need for adequate training is so obvious that failure to provide it is legally actionable. For example, the career of a common patrol officer presents the potential for use of deadly force in making arrests. Although application of deadly force may not be a usual and recurring situation with which he or she is faced, the patrol officer must nonetheless be adequately trained as to at least minimum constitutional standards governing such events. Given this recognition of a somewhat generic requirement for training in the careers of police generalists such as patrol officers, what then are the appropriate expectations and standards for training applicable to specialized tactical officers? Are not the usual and recurring situations and duties associated with these officers the sort which involve significantly higher probabilities of extreme danger and corresponding use of deadly force? Viewed in this manner, a failure of a police supervisor to provide the

---

1. Footnote 10, *City of Canton v. Harris*, reads in part: "For example, city policymakers know to a moral certainty that their police officers will be required to arrest fleeing felons....Thus, the need to train officers in the constitutional limits on the use of deadly force (see *Tennessee v. Garner* [1985]) can be said to be 'so obvious' that failure to do so could properly be characterized as deliberate indifference to constitutional rights."

additional training commensurate with these heightened risks may foster litigation from those who perceive themselves as harmed thereby (Mijares and Perkins, 1994, pp. 2-4). Such a perception as grounds for litigation finds support in the following specific language taken from ·Justice White's opinion in *Harris*:

> ....it may seem that in light of the duties assigned to specific officers or employees the need for more or different training is so obvious and the inadequacy so likely to result in the violation of constitutional rights, that the policy makers of the city can reasonably be said to have been deliberately indifferent to the need. In that event the failure to provide proper training may fairly be said to represent a policy for which the city is responsible if it actually causes harm (p.390).

Except for the rarest of agencies, virtually all officers are presumably now receiving the basic essential training in terms of limits in the use of deadly force. If such training is not occurring within a particular agency, individual tactical officers, their supervisors, and other executive officials within the local government entities are, unfortunately, imprudent in terms of litigation risk management. The suggestion offered here is that the training of tactical personnel go beyond the bare essentials that are suitable for a patrol officer. Training policies that are clearly adequate as opposed to only arguably adequate will help to create a more protective shield, not only for individual field tactical officers claiming good faith adherence to those policies, but also for their supervisors and employing governmental entities when called upon to defend any form of civil action (Alpert and Smith, 1990).

Chapter Five

ADVANCED TRAINING

In-service, follow-up, continuous—all of these descriptions of advanced training beyond the initial stage refer essentially to the same topic: the maintenance and continuous improvement of individual skill levels and the addition, adaptation, and coordination of team techniques after basic tactical training has been completed. Since the training needs of each law enforcement agency change on an almost daily basis, it would be meaningless and futile to offer a universal training program. This chapter will address the following issues of follow-up training for the veteran tactical officer:

1. Why train at all beyond the initial stage of tactical training, especially after successfully completing the rigorous initial tactical training described in the previous chapter?
2. What should be the substantive content of advanced tactical training?
3. What are the sources of training beyond the initial stage?
4. How often should advanced training take place?
5. How should training at this level be conducted with the maximum effect?

Previous studies of tactical training beyond the initial stage have tended to follow a generalized approach. Jacobs (1983) indicated that a final goal for the completion of tactical training should never be set. A tactical team should never be satisfied with the completion of a single training program. Since new ideas and methods are constantly being introduced, there is always room for improvement through continued training. The follow-up training process not only identifies performance shortcomings but also develops teamwork among members of the unit, promotes the introduction of experiments in technique and technology and allows the refinement of these innovations under controlled conditions.

A RATIONALE FOR CONTINUOUS TRAINING

Tactical training must be conducted without cease for several reasons. First, such training fulfills various legal requirements. As previously indicated, *City of Canton v. Harris* (1989) suggests how police departments are required to train personnel for the unique duties associated with the many specialized assignments of a law enforcement agency. Both *Canton* and common wisdom dictate that such training be continued throughout an officer's tenure in order to remain abreast of the times. Although more specific legal precedents are difficult to find defining the exact standards, continued training can logically be viewed as a legitimate measure to reduce allegations of misconduct for failure to train as well as a means to improve police service. In addition, advanced training is required by many of the various state law enforcement regulatory agencies in order to maintain certification as a police officer. In most instances, SWAT training sessions, when properly conducted and documented by competent instructional personnel, provide the training hours needed for continued law enforcement certification.

Follow-up training provides the opportunity to review and practice the tactics and techniques already learned during the initial stage of training. Professional athletes who are at the pinnacle of their performance levels must still practice the skills that made them champions. When a reporter referred to Arnold Palmer as a "lucky" golfer, the legendary player smiled, agreed, and expanded on the observation with his own statement that the more he practiced, the luckier he became. Luck may be defined then as the ability to recognize options and to prepare one's self to respond positively. Advanced tactical training increases options and improves the ability of a tactical unit to respond successfully. Thus, the repeated practice of existing skills under supervision should be an integral part of a follow-up training program.

Closely following the refinement of individual skills comes the transformation of singular police officers into an organized team. The "Dream Team" of the United States Olympic Basketball Program consisted of an assembly of some of the greatest players in the history of the game. Several months before actual competition began, they practiced together, not only to refine their individual skills but also to develop the organizational coordination needed to perform as a team.

The team's total domination of the opposition during the 1992 Olympic Games is legendary. Just as championship football, basketball, hockey, and baseball teams are the result of coordinated group efforts, successful tactical teams require coordinated, collective efforts. Thus, a vital objective of advanced tactical training is to transform a group of skilled and qualified, but often disjointed, police officers into a well-disciplined and highly coordinated unit and to maintain the unit integrity that is so important for successful mission accomplishment and fulfillment of organizational objectives and goals.

Advanced training sessions also provide the opportunity to examine, test, evaluate, and put into operation new equipment and techniques. To introduce new technology and methods during an actual tactical operation without adequate testing, preparation, and practice invites failure and subjects the agency to unnecessary civil litigation. More will be said about the roles of equipment and technology in Chapter Six.

All forms of police operations and the preparations for them should be re-evaluated on a regular basis to reflect changes in statutory and case law as well as trends in society and in criminal behavior. Individual and team weaknesses not addressed during the initial stage of training must also be identified and remedied during follow-up training. This aspect of training requires supervisory officers and the training staff to meet regularly with personnel involved in actual tactical operations for debriefing and constructive criticism. Previous cases must be reviewed and corrective measures must be initiated through the training process.

Follow-up tactical training must accomplish the above objectives and more. During any tactical training program the team leaders and training staff must constantly remind the trainees of the SWAT mission; i.e., to contain, control and de-escalate a special threat at minimal risk to police personnel and bystanders as well as to the criminal suspect. The measure of success of a tactical training program may be defined by the amount of force that can be avoided through an increase in options rather than through the amount of force that can be employed.

TRAINING CONTENT

Training for any specialized police assignment should be approached with the realization that substantive content is dependent on the specific needs of each department. Community conditions change on a daily basis and these changes take place in divergent directions and at different rates. Thus, a specific training program that may be beneficial for one police department may not necessarily be valid, relevant, or appropriate for another.

Tactical units should attempt to maintain proficiency and professionalism in several substantive areas of expertise at much higher levels of performance than expected of the remainder of the police force. Thus, advanced tactical training must first provide the time and opportunity for the addition and development of new knowledge, skills, and abilities. Individually, tactical officers should develop and maintain their skills and knowledge in such areas as armed and unarmed close-quarter confrontation techniques, less-lethal options, barricaded entry methods, and the safe handling of hazardous tools and materials. The fact that many, if not most, advanced tactical procedures use physically demanding and rapid movements and actions that are automatically coordinated demands training cycles that are frequent enough to maintain desired skill levels.

Consider, for example, the skills required to enter a structure for a high-risk warrant service on the part of one officer:

I. The officer should understand all laws and agency policies related to the service of the warrant as well as the procedures utilized for the operation.
II. The officer should be well trained in the use of:
   A. The primary weapon (usually a submachine gun or rifle)
   B. The secondary weapon (pistol)
   C. The operation of both weapons with lights attached
   D. All of the intricate manipulations of the weapons including, but not limited to:
      1. Accurate fire above 90% hit factor
      2. Speed reloading
      3. Tactical reloading
      4. Malfunction drills
      5. Transition drills

6. Failure drills

7. Hostage shots at various distances

8. Shooting on the move

9. Shooting while wounded (one-handed)

10. Shooting from various physical positions

11. Weapons retention (both weapons)

12. Cover fire–suppressive fire concepts

E. Downed officer/citizen rescue tactics

F. Emergency medical concepts

G. Use and deployment of:

1. Oleoresin capsicum (OC) spray

2. Flash/sound diversion devices

3. Tear gas

4. ASP baton

5. Gas mask

6. Breaching devices for both interior and exterior doors

H. Skills and concepts of preliminary negotiations

I. Entry movements including:

1. Cross over

2. Button hook

3. High/low

4. Stealth

5. Dynamic

6. Stacking at breach point

7. Interior flow to accommodate all changes in assignment that can occur when suspects are encountered or when officers are injured

III. Protecting crime scenes after a use of force or a shooting.

IV. Following after-incident procedures, including a de-briefing and critique.

These learned skills require redundancy to build muscle memory and the ability to perform these skills under great stress almost instinctively in split seconds. In any one incident it is a distinct possibility that a single officer may be required to perform almost every skill listed and do so in a time frame of seconds and minutes, not hours. Additional physical training is needed for the myriad other tasks associated with pursuing a violent criminal suspect, employing the appropriate level of force to stifle further criminal activity and securing the perpetrator to prevent escape, all while wearing heavy protective equipment that greatly inhibits mobility, reduces the usual full range of motion, and depletes normal energy reserves at an accelerated pace.

Associated with the acquisition and practice of skills is the ability to perform them under extremely stressful conditions with continuous changes in weather, lighting, work-induced fatigue, work areas (buildings, residential houses, apartments, schools, buses, planes, trains, etc.), technological advances, and societal changes. The content of advanced training should be the product of a ceaseless analysis of needs conducted by qualified training personnel to determine where, when, and under what conditions tactical operations in a particular area tend to occur. Tactical personnel should be trained in immediate-action responses to unprecedented and changing criminal behavior. For example, the particular aberrant actions of the criminal suspects during the North Hollywood Bank Incident defied exact tactical pre-planning. However, the actions taken by SWAT officers during the event were nonetheless immediate and decisive. Such efficiency is a classic example of a conditioned response which is largely the result of training in varied situations so intensely and frequently that even spontaneous reactions of the responding personnel appear to be automatic.

Further, an integral aspect of all advanced tactical training programs should be reference to the agency's published rules and regulations pertaining to the correct use of force. These documents are (or should be) shaped by the guidelines set forth in the seminal United States Supreme Court decisions in *Tennessee v. Garner* (1985) and *Graham v. Connor* (1989), as well as by off-spring cases from those decisions. Training in the use of force should include reference to department policy, state and federal legislation, and relevant litigation that guide official police response to potentially violent confrontations with the criminal element.

Next, the content of advanced tactical training should include the opportunity for the evaluation of the trainee's ability to retain and apply the information presented. The testing process not only examines the knowledge levels, skills, and abilities of the trainees, but also provides the organization with information about the instructional procedures being followed by the teaching staff. When properly documented, it also provides evidence of the law enforcement agency's intention to avoid the allegation of "deliberate indifference" to organizational training needs. Advanced training should include a review of various historical SWAT scenarios, both successful and unsuccessful. While not every situation is exactly the same, enough similarities can be drawn to allow thorough planning based on patterns of criminal behavior. Similarly, the recognition of differences can identify approaches to be avoided. Employing historical scenarios during training sessions will greatly expedite the planning process during an actual mission.

Finally, the SWAT team does not operate in a vacuum. In fact, the SWAT team is one of many parts within the overall police agency that must work in concert rather than conflict to bring about the safe and successful resolution of a tactical incident. During the North Hollywood Bank Incident, personnel from many different sections of the Los Angeles Police Department became involved. Although officers from the SWAT Team were responsible for the effective neutralization of one of the criminal subjects, officers from patrol, traffic control, homicide, and victim services were among the many responding units who played significant roles under the careful guidance of dispatchers from the communications division. Therefore, to enhance intraorganizational coordination it is important for the content of tactical training to involve other units of the law enforcement agency (Snow, 1996).

SOURCES OF FOLLOW UP TRAINING

Under the most ideal conditions, follow-up training should be conducted by a permanent training staff. Personnel assigned to the training staff are generally supervisory or senior tactical officers who have already demonstrated their qualifications and whose enthusiasm for the field of tactical operations is unquestionable. Such officers need not be the most accurate shots or the fastest runners or the best martial artists any more than the coach of a professional sports team must outperform any athlete to be a successful coach. Members of a tactical training staff must possess skills comparable to those of the coaching staff of a professional athletic team. They must be able to identify assets and liabilities in team talent. They must maximize strong points, strengthen weak points, and mold a collection of individuals into a cohesive and disciplined unit.

One form of follow-up training consists of regularly scheduled qualification courses (firearms, physical fitness, classroom, etc.). Satisfactory performance at posted standards is a requirement of some tactical units to remain a unit member in good standing (Treusch, 1991). Requiring members to achieve satisfactory performance at an established level is also a legal criterion to maintain governmental immunity from negligence litigation (Schmidt, 1976).

A second form of advanced training is usually the result of research conducted by the training staff on a needs basis. For example, the training staff may be called upon to formulate the tactical plans for the deployment of personnel during the visit of a dignitary. Advanced training allows the team members to reduce the range of possibilities for error to the lowest level and to execute the operation without incident. This type of training calls for a progressive improvement in efficiency and speed by team members through controlled "dry run" rehearsals, critiques of performance, and continuous practice under conditions that simulate reality as closely as possible.

Third, advanced training can be provided by the manufacturers and distributors of tactical products. Manufacturers such as Smith and Wesson and Def-tec Corporation provide a wide variety of training programs to familiarize police personnel in the proper use and maintenance of their respective products. Instruction in these fields is provided by the actual developers of the products and is generally limited to the technical aspects of their use.

Proprietary operations provide a fourth source and form of advanced training. Staffed by instructors whose technical expertise and actual experience may vary widely, these operations offer a quality of instruction in an equally wide range. Of equal importance to the police administrator are the actual relevance and cost effectiveness of these programs. The experienced administrator will soon discover that many of these programs are overpriced "dog-and-pony shows" of questionable merit and relevance to actual law enforcement needs. In many cases they are repetitive and are more concerned with presenting the skills that trainees enjoy doing more than the topics that tactical officers must know as they employ a "take the money and run" approach. Close checking of references and conferring with the state law enforcement training council should be done before using these outside sources. Of particular concern are the proprietary operations with solely a military or foreign background. While these sources may provide excellent skill training, some of these trainers have presented the material in a manner from a perspective not reflecting a domestic law enforcement context.

Tactical expertise can also be found through governmental agencies such as the Federal Bureau of Investigation (FBI) and the Federal Law Enforcement Training Center (FLETC) in Glynco, Georgia. Training programs provided by the FBI may be arranged by contacting the Bureau's nearest regional office while FLETC may be called directly for information regarding specific training programs.

Various professional organizations such as the International Association of Chiefs of Police (IACP) and the National Tactical Officers Association also offer training programs directly applicable to the needs of tactical officers. In addition, statewide and regional associations of tactical officers exist for the same purpose. This coursework is much less costly than that offered by proprietary operations. In some cases it is free. High-quality instruction is provided by active and retired tactical officers who not only possess impressive credentials but also have already demonstrated their expertise in the field. The very nature of these programs allows the use of innovative training techniques such as role playing and team competition. More importantly, they allow an exchange of ideas and mutual constructive criticism.

On the whole, professional associations of police tactical personnel have followed the lead of several different traditional professional associations. Just as organizations such as the American Medical Association and the American Bar Association have their state, regional, and national chapters, the National Tactical Officers Association and 14 state and regional associations[1] have encouraged significant contributions to the body of knowledge about tactical operations by endorsing legitimate research projects and by sponsoring regularly scheduled conferences and specific training programs to disseminate the organized information resulting from that research. In 1998 the NTOA counted approximately 20,000 individuals and 600 teams as its members. Similarly, the Texas Tactical Police Officers Association is composed of approximately 1200 individuals from over 70 teams as members.

---

1. California, Florida, Illinois, Iowa, Michigan, Mountain States, Mississippi, North Carolina, Ohio, South Carolina, Southeast Region, Texas, Virginia, and Washington.

National and state associations of police tactical officers have carried this concept of training even further and enhanced the learning process by providing the opportunity to apply newly developed and often theoretical information to a practical problem and solution. The training session and the application period are followed by a constructive critique.

However, for several reasons which do not lend themselves to rational and empirical explanations, conferences and training sessions sponsored by associations of police tactical personnel tend to be attended primarily by rank-and-file patrol officers. Unless the topic of a conference is specifically germane to the management of tactical units, attendance by persons in leadership positions is usually relatively low. Thus, it has become incumbent upon police professional associations to provide training media and opportunities not only for the personnel performing specific law enforcement tasks but also for the supervisors and managers of these operations who are ultimately responsible for achieving organizational goals and objectives.

This sort of training must be undertaken with a degree of caution. Many of these courses are conducted with participants from several different law enforcement agencies. As a result of the generalized approach taken to accommodate the wide variety of participants in this form of training, all trainees, especially those who are supervisory officers, must often modify the substance of this training to meet the specific needs of their respective departments.

Finally, training can take place in a very effective way through mutual aid agreements that exist among geographically close law enforcement agencies. Expenses for training and operations for only one agency may be financially prohibitive and the reassignment of nontactical personnel to maintain the patrol force may unduly retard the response time for normal calls for police service. Mutual aid agreements allow the concerned departments to share resources, facilities, and personnel in a cost-effective manner. Even without formalized mutual aid agreements it has become common for some agencies to modify this concept by allowing their tactical units to participate in joint training operations on a less-formal basis. The demands for this sort of training require each officer to become a trainer as well as a trainee. Each participant is forced to assume a more active role in the overall training process.

Irrespective of the source of the training, the management of the law enforcement agency is responsible for assuring that the individuals conducting the training are qualified to teach a given subject and that they possess the proper credentials. To maintain an instructional staff that is less than adequate may easily be construed as maintaining a mental state ranging from simple negligence all the way to deliberate indifference. This condition intensifies the risk of litigation. Before a possible instructor is given consideration to be part of any training staff, law enforcement management could apply the same criteria as that which is applied to expert witnesses in courtroom testimony:

1. What sort of practical experience is possessed by the potential instructor?
2. What sort of relevant training and education has the potential instructor pursued?

Resumes, professional experience, and claimed expertise of any outside instructors should be checked and verified. Instructors with criminal histories or alliances that would embarrass the agency should be rejected. In addition, the instructional staff should possess sufficient teaching skills and the needed oratory ability to conduct classes at this level.

· In spite of the fact that only one state (Montana) requires satisfactory completion of a specific course of study to become SWAT officers, tactical personnel tend to undergo more frequent and more rigorous training than most other types of police officers. Because of the many continuous changes in this dynamic field of law enforcement, SWAT trainers must assume several roles (Mijares and Perkins, 1998).

First, *SWAT trainers must be teachers.* To assume this role they must do more than possess substantive knowledge in a wide range of SWAT-related topics. They must also possess the necessary experience to apply this knowledge in a variety of settings with a diversity of students. In addition, they must be well versed in the language and art of instruction. They must know the music that goes with the words. They must be able to determine the specific learning objectives that must be accomplished to gain the skills, behaviors, and knowledge areas desired in a tactical officer. And, like other teachers, the SWAT instructor must maintain a gradebook. A review of *Langford v. Gates* (1987) indicates that documentation of all phases of training and field execution is critical. Recorded successful experiences may well equate to subsequent judicial approval of tactical operations. Obviously this phase of the training process includes the maintenance of records of the progress of each individual student and of the test results achieved through both training and actual field applications of particular strategies, equipment, etc.

· Second, *SWAT trainers must be coaches.* Training a SWAT team is much like coaching a professional sports team. SWAT personnel are much like professional athletes, often already possessing a relatively high skill level and, because of the youth factor, usually possessing more raw strength and endurance than the coach. Like the coach, the SWAT instructor must keep the students motivated and constantly mindful that they are more than a group of individuals and that SWAT operations are successful only when everyone treats them as team operations.

Third, *the SWAT instructor must become a researcher.* Additions and revisions to existing legislation, new judicial interpretations, improvements in techniques, and innovations in police product technology have taken place in quantum leaps. Keeping informed of these changes and identifying appropriate training objectives is a full-time job. This job requires skills in issue identification, data collection and analysis, and decision making based on accepted scientific research methods. Consequently, it will be incumbent on the SWAT instructor to seek the information needed actively to enhance the delivery of SWAT services. Some relevant information is available through media such as *The Tactical Edge* and *Command.* These journals are published on a quarterly basis only after a lengthy review of the articles submitted. There are numerous other publications that on occasion are SWAT-specific in approach and content. These sources can often provide generalized research that can be applied by analogy to SWAT operations.

Finally, while SWAT instructors need not be attorneys, *they should become familiar with the relevant court decisions and legislation that affect tactical training and operations* (pp. 9-10). The department legal advisor should be consulted by instructors and executives on a regular basis on matters pertaining to civil liability and the potential for litigation concerning training issues. Departments that are too small to employ a full-time legal advisor often retain a local attorney for this purpose or they may share an attorney with other departments through their membership in a regional council of government or in a statewide municipal league. Since attorneys affiliated with state professional associations of tactical police officers are primarily charged with providing legal counsel for the association, their ability to serve in this capacity for individual departments may be restricted. Attorneys employed by local prosecutors are fundamentally concerned with criminal prosecutions and, therefore, may possess limited experience and expertise in the specialized area of police civil litigation.

TRAINING FREQUENCY

The frequency of follow-up training is also a matter of wide variation among police agencies. At one extreme are the departments that fail to provide any time at all for advanced training beyond the initial stage. The reasons for this failure are many, and the legal, practical, and ethical ramifications of this practice become obvious.

At the other extreme, many of the European police agencies follow a military approach by remaining in a constant training mode when not involved in a tactical operation. It can actually be counterproductive for a police officer to be removed from the street for an extended period of time even for training purposes. When a police officer loses contact with the conditions of the street and with his or her network of street informants, a failure to recognize the subtle changes that take place in his or normal area of patrol can occur. Most importantly, the intangible "feel" for the street is often lost. From the training perspective, the drawbacks to this approach far outweigh the benefits. Trainees easily become bored and stale when their skills are developed but never tested under actual tactical conditions.

Some tactical units allow one or two hours per day for physical training (e.g., Houston Police SWAT, Los Angeles Police SWAT, Los Angeles County Sheriff's Office SWAT, and Maricopa County, Arizona Sheriff's Office SWAT). However, this option may not be feasible in part-time tactical operations or in small departments where the tactical assignment is secondary.

An ideal approach is to allocate three to five days of the work month for advanced training purposes. This approach would allow the tactical officer to devote the majority of time to the demands of the non-tactical assignment while maintaining the individual and team skills necessary for tactical operations. Equally important, regularly scheduled training would aid the attempt to avoid media criticism and the unwelcome civil litigation that often follows the implementation of operations during an actual tactical operation. However, such an amount is unrealistic for most departments and remains a goal for which tactical teams should strive.

ENHANCING THE TRAINING EFFECT

Training can be a drudgery or it can be a stimulant. It can be an exercise in futility and a waste of time or it can be an effective means of individual and organizational improvement and a wise use of departmental resources in which long-term benefits far outweigh short-term expenses and inconveniences.

Snow (1996) suggests several means of enhancing the effects of advanced tactical training. First, training should be as realistic as possible. While it may not be feasible for every tactical unit to construct a live-fire shooting facility comparable to the facilities possessed by West Germany's GSG-9, the use of paintball weapons and other variations of technology provide sufficient simulation of actual tactical situations. The scenarios used in tactical training should replicate the situations that have already been experienced and should approximate conditions likely to be encountered. These conditions include lighting, weather, geography, and time. In addition, since police officers tend to overact when role playing in simulations, Snow recommends that actors from drama classes or community theaters be utilized.

Second, training should be more demanding than any expected actual operations. This condition can be introduced by adding stressors to the training session. Some SWAT units, such as the Austin Police Department Special Missions Force have found that since any type of stressor—physical, mental, or emotional—can affect the ability to function at peak performance, adding some sort of extreme physical exertion prior to the instructional session or requiring the trainees to perform a series of mental mathematical computations during a scenario can complicate the training exercise in such a way that the application of the practiced techniques to an actual situation is relatively less difficult.

Third, Snow also suggests that the tactical training is not just for SWAT personnel. Since members of the patrol force are usually the first responders to most hostile situations, it is extremely important for these officers to understand their own roles and what is required before the arrival of the SWAT unit. Other units that have roles at critical incidents also should be included in the training. In addition to departmental units such as hostage negotiators, traffic control personnel, victim counselors, and dispatchers, units outside the department such the local fire department, emergency medical services personnel, and even representatives from the public utility companies, the news media, and local government should be included.

Similarly, it is important for the command structure to understand the SWAT role and its capabilities, responsibilities, and limitations. Particular attention should be paid to issues such as the department's position on chain of command and unity of command.

A fourth training enhancement technique, which is not mentioned by Snow but is gaining more acceptance, is mutual observation by representatives from other tactical units. The observing visitors gain from this approach by learning alternatives that may have been overlooked in their own training while the team being observed gains from constructive criticism.

Fifth, training can and should be enhanced by accentuating the positive and avoiding instruction by negation. This principle of instruction was pointed out in *Sager v. City of Woodland Park* (1982) where local officers were sent to an outside agency for training. During the course an example was used to demonstrate how *not* to conduct a particular operation. Apparently, when the officers returned to their parent command, as a result of confusion arising out of their training exercise, they mistakenly followed the procedure which they were told to avoid.

Finally, many tactical units have improved training efficacy by adding the element of competition. State and national conferences of specialized police officers often sponsor competition in conjunction with their business meetings and information sessions (Mullins and Mijares, 1994). These competitions provide participants with networking opportunities for information sharing, constructive criticism given with strong encouragement, alternatives to currently employed tactics and techniques, and specific goals for practice sessions. As a side benefit, the hosting police agency often develops a training facility that would otherwise be nonexistent.

CASE HISTORY: THE NORTH HOLLYWOOD BANK
OF AMERICA INCIDENT

On February 28, 1997, at approximately 9:15 a.m., two heavily armed men approached the Bank of America at 6600 Laurel Canyon Boulevard at Archwood Street. Upon entering the bank the suspects, later identified as Emil Matasareanu and Larry Eugene Phillips, ordered all of the bank's employees and customers to the floor. This order was accomplished as the suspects both brandished and fired fully automatic weapons of both the AK-47 and M-16 categories. Following the confiscation of literally a cartload of cash, the suspects herded the bank employees and patrons into the bank vault and began their escape (Leovy and Chu, 1997; King, 1997). Meanwhile, in response to reports of the robbery in progress, numerous police officers had arrived outside and established a containing perimeter outside the bank. Other patrol officers were situated in the surrounding area, closing off streets and ordering occupants to remain inside their homes, schools, and businesses (Blankstein and Bernstein, 1997). As the gunmen emerged from the bank, they were engaged by the patrol officers who were armed only with handguns and shotguns. Several officers, recognizing their inability to neutralize the pair, borrowed rifles and ammunition from a North Hollywood gun shop (Davis, 1997).

At the time of the incident, members of the Los Angeles Police Department's SWAT team were attending a training session at the Police Academy approximately sixteen miles from the crime scene. Dispatched directly from the academy and briefed while en route, some arrived still clad in workout attire (Shuster and Rainey, 1997). The balance in firepower previously existing was, however, finally neutralized with their ability to bring their own weapons (MP-5 submachine guns and CAR-15 carbines) to bear (Johnson, 1997). Eventually, despite continuous gunfire from the suspects, officers from SWAT Van Nuys and North Hollywood conducted separate rescues of both fellow officers and civilians, accomplishing one such rescue by commandeering an armored truck and using it as a ballistic shield and evacuation vehicle (Shuster, 1997).

In addition to newspaper accounts, live television images and videotapes captured the event as it unfolded and provided further and even more graphic details (Davis, 1997). These sources began their coverage as the suspects moved from the bank's entry area and approached a white sedan which they had positioned as a "getaway" car. Suspect Matasareanu took a position behind the steering wheel, but for reasons that will forever remain unknown, Phillips did not join him in the car. Instead, he continued on foot following his partner east on Archwood as though he preferred to take a leisurely stroll through the residential neighborhood firing his weapon at random targets. Phillips is clearly seen being struck by bullets fired by police officers. However, the ballistic protection covering his legs and torso allowed him to continue walking in the open and firing. He was eventually fatally wounded, apparently by a combination of police fire and a self-inflicted shot from his own handgun.

Meanwhile, three SWAT officers had initiated a pursuit of Matasareanu in their marked police vehicle. These officers subsequently encountered the suspect at a location where he had attempted to abandon his crippled vehicle and commandeer a pickup truck from a passing citizen. It is at this point where evidence of effective tactical training becomes apparent.

The driver of the police vehicle positioned the unit in such a manner as to both block escape and apparently to utilize the pickup's engine block as a ballistic shield. Meanwhile the officer in the front seat leaned from the window to generate a base of cover fire to force the suspect down. The driver and the officer in the rear seat exited the police vehicle as the cover fire was continued toward the suspect who now had taken a position at the rear of the white sedan. Apparently unable to see the suspect clearly over the sedan, the officers crawled under the police car in a prone position and began firing at the suspect's ankles and feet.

Simultaneous with the three officers' firefight with the suspect, it is obvious that other responding police personnel continued to engage the suspect from other directions. Their actions created a diversion and drew the suspect's fire from the SWAT officers. When the suspect appeared to be unable to continue firing his weapon, one of the SWAT officers displayed a hand signal to cease fire, thus allowing the SWAT officers to approach and secure the suspect and the crime scene.

The North Hollywood Bank of America Incident demonstrated the relationship between continuous tactical training and organizational success in several ways. First and foremost, continuous training helps develop the relevant knowledge bases, skills, and abilities of the responding officers to a high operational level. From start to finish the incident required a high level of physical and mental endurance which continuous training tends to promote. In addition, the officers' familiarity and competence with the technology at their disposal was possible only through advanced training.

Closely related, the intra- and extraorganizational training regularly practiced by the Los Angeles SWAT unit resulted in an extraordinarily high level of automatic coordination of efforts, particularly with the patrol division. The reaction by all units responding to the scene could not have been written any better by a script writer. Despite the speed with which the incident took place, traffic units immediately kept innocent bystanders from entering the fields of fire. Investigative units stepped in at appropriate times to preserve crime scenes and to reinforce and relieve patrol and SWAT units so that the uniformed officers could resume their apprehension and rescue operations until it was certain that no other perpetrators were involved. Coordination of the responses of the sort displayed is indicative of the composure on the part of dispatchers and other communications personnel who provided critical information, organized and arranged the movement of personnel and equipment, and in general served as the important conduit between individual officers and the rest of the department. Such coordination is the result of more than written policies deeming it to be so. It is the result of practice, discipline, and familiarity by each participant in the duties, strengths, and limitations of each component part of such a critical operation.

Third, a desired effect of continuous advanced tactical training is the development of the ability to make adjustments during the course of the response. Throughout the event the police were continuously confronted with unprecedented and, therefore, unpredictable behavior. A failure to have previously developed the ability to make adjustments to changing conditions could have been disastrous.

Finally, the practice associated with advanced training results in high levels of initiative and the ability to follow proper procedures without prodding. The discipline and self-restraint needed to achieve this condition is not due solely to even the strongest of leadership. These characteristics are the result of good training, constructive criticism, effective feedback, and predictability of action by all participants in the operation. This fact implies that all responding personnel, regardless of rank, are totally familiar with established departmental, unit, and individual procedures that must be followed during these events. It also implies that the supervisor has been a major factor in the advanced training to see the performance of subordinates under simulated stressful scenarios and to allow the patrol officers to observe leadership under similar conditions. Responding police personnel should not require detailed instructions of their assigned duties during these critical incidents. Their responses should be automatic.

Chapter Six

EQUIPMENT

The acronym, *SWAT* (Special Weapons and Tactics), has traditionally suggested the police use of sophisticated weaponry to overcome unusually violent, well-equipped, technically proficient, and
highly motivated criminals. However, many times the perpetrators of
incidents requiring more than a routine police response have enjoyed
the element of surprise, fortified positions, and numerical advantage.
Thus, at times the police response has been hindered by limited physical assets, restrained by a genuine concern for the safety of victims
and innocent bystanders, and impeded by an inability to gain useful
information concerning the exact location, condition, and activities of
the perpetrator. American law enforcement does not operate in the
free-fire zones of declared wars, nor can any level of casualties be considered acceptable. The automatic introduction of an all-out conventional military response to a situation such as a barricaded suspect
would be counterproductive to the long-term mission of American law
enforcement.

Advancements in the technology available to the police have resulted in law enforcement's limited ability to employ graduated responses, at least in certain instances. Not as "headline grabbing" as the big
shootout, but categorically to be preferred, the likelihood of a peacefully negotiated surrender has been enhanced through such developments. Of course some scenarios simply defy a purely technological
solution. Also, as we shall see, the use of some forms of technologies
in the surveillance category give rise to other important debates on the
legitimate parameters of police intrusion into personal privacy.
Constitutional issues have arisen in the attempt to strike an appropriate balance between societal security and the protection of individual
rights.

In many instances the advances in available police equipment have come from modifying the developments in other fields and applying these developments to immediate law enforcement needs and are intended to increase the number of options available for police response through an expansion of the use-of-force continuum, enhanced intelligence-gathering methods, and improved officer protection. Thus, after summarizing the historical development of police tactical equipment, this chapter will address the following:

1. An identification of the various types and sources of equipment designed to give tactical units more effective technological choices which produce an ability to use fatal force only as a final option. This discussion will include a rationale for each piece of equipment and will in some specific instances make references to questions of law regarding when and under what circumstances the equipment may be used.

2. A description of the alternatives to conventional purchasing procedures by which the limited budgets imposed on most tactical units can be expanded.

3. A realistic projection of the future developments in the field of police tactical equipment.

THE EVOLUTION OF INDIVIDUAL POLICE TACTICAL EQUIPMENT

Even the least sophisticated of today's SWAT teams possesses equipment that generally exceeds the quality of its parent police agency. The original SWAT teams were outfitted in machine washable utility uniforms and baseball caps to allow more mobility than the amount allowed by a traditional police uniform. In many cases the utility uniform was not designed specifically for the wear and tear of law enforcement, as some SWAT officers took the appearance of jump-suited gas station attendants. Footwear was often an industrial work boot or a military boot originally designed for use in Viet Nam.

Shoulder weapons ranged from pump shotguns to fully automatic M-16 rifles. Some tactical units carried M-1, .30 caliber carbines made available through the National Rifle Association's Director of Civilian Marksmanship. Handguns could range from an American made .38 Special revolver to a .45 caliber military Model 1911 A1 Pistol. Less lethal munitions only consisted of variations of tear gas, either thrown by hand after activating a Bouchon fuse, or fired from a single-shot 37 millimeter launcher (gas gun).

Surveillance equipment was limited to hand-held mirrors, often removed from the handlebars of bicycles belonging to officers' children. Some enterprising officers invested in dental mirrors to enhance portability. Communications equipment was so heavy, limited in its transmission and reception capabilities, and unreliable when used indoors or around electrical lines that it was often cast aside in favor of hand signals. Equipment vehicles were secondhand delivery trucks which were often modified and painted by the officers without the necessary financial assistance from the police department.

At the least, today's SWAT team is dressed in tear-resistant battle dress utility uniforms (BDUs) of varying colors according to climate, environment, and geography. Where the original utility uniforms were available only in the olive drab found in Army-Navy surplus stores, several manufacturers have recognized the need for the tactical officers of contemporary urban law enforcement to adopt a less militaristic appearance and to look more like civilian police officers.

Recognizing the potential for flash fires when serving warrants in illegal drug processing laboratories, a growing number of tactical units are outfitted in utility uniforms made from flame-resistant Nomex® fabric. Available in both one-piece and conventional two-piece designs, these uniforms are tailored in the same manner as the original utility uniform, complete with cargo pockets and closures as well as reinforced and padded knees, elbows, and seats. A relatively limited number of teams have even ordered long underwear made from similar material to give the same protection enjoyed by professional drivers on the NASCAR and CART automobile racing circuits. Nomex gloves and balaclavas complete the protection from fire[1] and caustic chemicals.

The original utility uniform was made to be worn in moderate climates. Today's police officer may work in the sub-zero and wet weather of winter in northern cities. Consequently, tactical officers working outdoors in these areas may wear utility uniforms made with a Gore-Tex® outer layer to provide protection against the elements while allowing the evaporation of body moisture. This clothing feature is made possible by employing a synthetic fabric so tightly woven that

---

1. The uniforms described here will not allow an individual to stay in a fire indefinitely. Anyone wearing such apparel in a fire will still endure a very high level of discomfort and can easily be overcome by smoke, fumes, and heat. These uniforms are primarily designed to protect against flashburns and allow the wearer to exit the premises immediately without the clothing combustion that would result from wearing cotton and polyester uniforms.

water molecules cannot penetrate, yet water vapor can evaporate. Polypropylene long underwear, which wicks moisture from the body, provides further protection against wet and cold weather.

Many manufacturers have developed footwear specifically designed for police tactical applications. Orthotically designed much like an athletic shoe with traction-providing soles and made from durable fabric and leather upper combinations that allow heat dissipation in the summer and warmth in the winter, these boots are easily maintained, comfortable, stable, and functional while offering an appropriate civilian appearance.

The MP-5 submachine gun, made by Germany's Heckler and Koch, is generally considered to be the shoulder weapon of choice. However, many police departments have elected to purchase less expensive weapons as a wide assortment of automatic and semi-automatic carbines, rifles, and shotguns remain in the law enforcement armory. Similarly, a wide variety of American and European handguns, too numerous to list in a single volume of this scope, in varying calibers are carried by SWAT teams throughout the country. In step with the movement to semi-automatic pistols has been a gradual move to larger caliber handgun rounds. Over the past ten years incidents of deadly force have all too often seen multiple shots fired with little immediate effect upon the suspect. Examinations of these incidents have led to the conclusion that increased velocity and increased bullet weight of at least 150 grains is necessary to stop threats quickly and reduce the number of shots fired by the police.

The extremely wide variation in type, quality, and price of individual police tactical equipment precludes a "one size fits all" approach to acquisition. Further, the differences in need, application, political influences, and budgetary limitations prevent the recommendation of specific purchases.

NEW DEVELOPMENTS IN TACTICAL EQUIPMENT

Contemporary SWAT teams have evolved from an accent on unusual and sometimes exotic weaponry to an emphasis on tactics and life-preserving technology. This evolution has largely been influenced by court decisions, community standards, and the recognition by criminal justice academics and practitioners alike that technology in many and varying fields has grown dramatically and that with creative and insightful minds this technology can be applied directly to tactical situations. It cannot be overstated that the most important factor contributing to the successful resolution of a tactical incident is the human element, complete with the necessary selection, training, and discipline associated with the staffing function of organizational management. However, there can be no doubt that the increase in technical options has resulted in an improved ability of tactical units to resolve complex and extremely violent situations with a decrease in casualties among victims, bystanders, police, and even the criminal suspects who initiate these hostile actions.

Increasing Options Through Less-Lethal Weaponry[2]

Traditionally, law enforcement officers who were required to use force were limited to very little between the risky and very often unpredictable use of a nightstick and a total commitment to the lethal force of a firearm. While tear gas has been in the police arsenal for several years, today's technology has begun to introduce a small additional number of graduated responses which allow the officer to complete a mission while keeping all risk factors to a minimum. One of these innovations bears special attention.

One of the most hazardous procedures of law enforcement operations is the neutralization of a barricaded suspect's activities, especially when hostages are involved. During the noise, excitement, and confusion of a rescue operation, hostages may not hear, understand, or heed the directions of rescuing law enforcement personnel. They may attempt to flee from the scene and become caught in a crossfire between rescue forces and the hostage takers.

Various law enforcement and military technicians recognized this likelihood in the early 1970s when hostage seizures became an international epidemic. They also recognized the need to devise a method to incapacitate both the hostages and the hostage takers temporarily without permanent injury until rescue personnel could safely take all parties into custody for proper identification, treatment, and legal disposition. Such incapacitation would require the physical neutralization and inability of everyone within the inner perimeter to move.

---

2. Originally presented by authors Mijares and Perkins at the 1995 meeting of the Academy of Criminal Justice Sciences in Boston, Mass., parts of the commentary in this section later appeared in the fall 1995 issue of *Police Liability Review* (pp. 1-8).

A nonfragmenting hand-delivered device later called a "Flash Bang,"[2] was developed to meet this need. Activated by a standard Bouchon fuse with a one-second delay, the device was composed of a cardboard canister containing a mixture of magnesium and gunpowder which, when ignited by the fuse, would immediately produce 20,000 footcandles of light and approximately 220 decibels of explosive noise. Flash/sound diversion devices used by contemporary American law enforcement are specifically designed to produce less than 180 decibels. This level is accepted as noninjurious to the human ear. The flash factor of most diversion devices used in domestic law enforcement is approximately 1,000,000 candela. American SWAT teams also place emphasis on the careful and safe placement of the device to reduce the already small potential for injury to any party.

It can be said that the primary reason to utilize flash/sound diversion devices is to prevent the likelihood of a shooting occurring by introducing an additional option that is less than a commitment to full lethality. The use of diversion devices should be controlled through written department guidelines and authorization from the SWAT commander. The majority of diversion devices give off a significant amount of smoke upon deflagration. The use of more than two or three devices in one location can significantly inhibit the ability of the SWAT team members to see.

A person exposed to the use of such a device will experience a temporary loss of hearing and vision. In addition, the combination of rapidly moving compressed air and physically shocking sound waves will instantly produce vertigo and disorientation. Depending on individual physiological differences and proximity to the exploding device, these effects will last from eight to twenty-two seconds. Even at the low end of this range rescue personnel can gain a tactical advantage and an opportunity to finalize the operation safely and without significant or permanent injury to themselves, to hostages, or to hostage takers.

The efficacy of this device was demonstrated on October 18, 1977, when members of West Germany's GSG-9 were called to Mogadishu, Somalia. In this instance a terrorist group had seized a Lufthansa Boeing 737 and issued several demands in exchange for the release of

---

2. These devices have also been called "Stun Grenades," "Thunder Flash Grenades," and "Diversionary Devices." The currently accepted term in the law enforcement community is "Less Lethal Munitions."

passengers. After being refused permission to land at several airports throughout Africa, the plane was finally allowed to land at the Mogadishu Airport. The pilot was killed and the terrorists repeated their demands with the threat that passengers and the remaining crew members also would be killed if the demands were not met.

When the government of Somalia realized the limitations of its own security forces, GSG-9 was requested to assume command of the situation. Operation "Magic Fire" began with the rescue personnel approaching the aircraft from the rear under the cover of darkness. Rubber-coated ladders were placed against the wings and fuselage of the plane. At a pre-arranged time the doors of the aircraft were opened simultaneously. Without any verbal warning or instructions, several diversionary devices were deployed and entry was made immediately. Passengers, crew, and terrorists alike were unable to move, and within seconds the rescue force was able to neutralize all threats (Tophoven, Verlag, and Verlag, 1984).

The "less-lethal" flash/sound option discussed above affords an opportunity to examine on a broader level the murky legalistic waters concerning other police choices of weaponry and the parties and circumstances surrounding its use. Until there is an honest admission that police are given little effective advance guidance on the appropriate use of force, charges of its misuse are likely to continue (Bitner, 1983). Quite simply, there are very few instances in which the courts have supplied concrete, fact-specific guidance on what types of strategies and/or equipment technology is relevant and proper to reduce the risk of human harm to a legally safe and yet operationally acceptable minimum. Police are thus left to examine a wide variety of case decisions involving either actual or potential life-threatening encounters, but with only generalized expressions within the opinions as to whether some specifically recognized alternative to the use of deadly force was or was not mandatory in a particular situation. Suffice it to say that in the current litigious environment of the times, there is ample enough vague, quasi-precedential case law for supervisors of tactical units to feel the need to explore the use of less-lethal force at every opportunity.

Because firearms are inherently lethal, they are justified only in the most extreme conditions of immediate threat to human life. It must also be foreseen that shots fired at an assailant may miss or pass through the target or ricochet, so that while intended to disable the assailant, they may instead have dire consequences for the innocent (Waddington, 1990). Paradoxically, for police tactical units operating in the types of situations necessitating their mobilization, incapacitation of assailants must be both total and immediate. To do otherwise arguably allows them the opportunity to open fire at either police officers, hostages, or other innocent bystanders or to detonate an explosive device even after being hit themselves. The circumstances are so extreme, with no room for error, that to consider inflicting less than instant and complete incapacitation (i.e., deadly force) upon an assailant merely transfers the risk of death to the innocent.

To what extreme a situation must rise or thereafter remain before tactical units can finally justify applications of deadly force is a question that may be fraught with specters of civil liability. Since immediate and grave decisions will become necessary during armed encounters, the dangers to innocent individuals can only be minimized by tactics that seek to avoid all-out confrontations. Planning should be based upon the highest quality of intelligence and training available. Advance considerations regarding the appropriate inventory of tactical weaponry to maintain on hand for use by the unit and its proper deployment is an imperative of liability risk management by police administrators.

In *Graham v. Connor* (1989) the Supreme Court redefined the standard by which claims of excessive force by the police are assessed and held that they are better analyzed under the Fourth Amendment's "objective reasonableness standard" rather than by reference to the Fourteenth Amendment's due process requirements. Prior to *Graham*, the Court had considered the reasonableness of seizures involving use of force within the context of the fleeing felon doctrine (*Tennessee v. Garner*, 1985). *Graham*, however, went further in that it expanded the scope of inquiry as to reasonableness into other types of seizure episodes and elaborated upon a totality of such circumstances as the severity of the crime at issue, whether the suspect imposes an immediate threat to the safety of officers or others, and whether there is active resistance to arrest (Hess, 1993). Accordingly, all use of force by police officers during arrest processes must be reasonable under the circumstances.

While the Court stated in *Graham* that it did not wish to create a judicial environment for unfairly second-guessing police arrest conduct, the inquiry into the reasonableness of police use of force nonetheless remains rooted in attention to all attendant factors. According to this approach, not just the actions of the assailant but also the alternatives that may be available to the police should be considered in evaluating the degree of force permissible to effectuate capture, while at the same time ensuring the safety of both officers and bystanders (Statchen, 1992). When applied to police tactical units and their arsenals, this approach would seem to beg some obvious additional inquiries. Given the fact that these units are typically formed and mobilized in anticipation of a need for specialized use of force, should legal assessment of their performance include stringent analysis of various alternative weaponry that might be available to them? In short, should there exist within this field of specialization a minimum standard of advance preparedness under which new and technologically superior "optional force" must be procured and tactical personnel adequately trained in its use? One of the fundamental backdrops for imposing tort liability has always been foreseeability of harm. Within the context of the so-called "constitutional torts," among the harms that both plaintiff categories (assailant and bystander) described herein may assert as being foreseeable is the deprivation of their Fourth Amendment rights accomplished through police failure to employ technologically less intrusive means of seizure.

As might be expected, the majority of the litigation directed at the general police population's alleged use of excessive force involves plaintiffs who are law breakers themselves. Therefore, a majority of the legal commentary revolves around police attempts to arrest them. Even harming acknowledged terrorists and criminals can, under certain circumstances, create negative consequences for law enforcement officials. An example of this phenomenon is the filing of a lawsuit in federal court against the Los Angeles Police Department, alleging that one of the suspects in the North Hollywood bank robbery (Chapter Five) was denied medical attention. The televised actions of the heavily armed suspects left no doubt that a violent crime of incredible proportions was taking place. The overall performance of the police was applauded by most. Nonetheless, in a free and open society, criticism and legal action can result.

Police defendants would logically prefer trial face-offs with this category of plaintiffs rather than bystanders, because from both legal and emotional perspectives assailants are less problematic to deal with. If an assailant threatens the officer or others with a weapon or where there is probable cause to believe that a crime has been committed involving the infliction of serious harm, then the United States Supreme Court has virtually presumed the existence of danger to society. However, this does not necessarily end all legal inquiry. The objective of such litigation is to divert both attention and liability from the criminal to the police.[3]

The bystander version of potential plaintiff presents some, but not all, of the same questions for resolution of liability. The situations wherein innocent parties are harmed while police tactical units are engaged in the arrest of assailants are likely to be termed by the officers as "collateral damage" or "accidental" inflictions of force and harm. When bystanders or hostages consider themselves to be the victims of excessive police force aimed not at them, but rather at assailants, the Supreme Court has determined that at least three amendments protect an individual's constitutional right to personal security: the Fourth, Fourteenth, and Eighth Amendments (Urbonya, 1993).

If the plaintiff's most desired targets are police supervisors, policymakers, or governmental entities, the majority of courts have required proof of a pattern or custom of harm-causing police action (translated a "policy") indicative of a higher degree of disregard than simply negligent behavior. Certainly *City of Canton v. Harris* (1989) stands for the premise that with regard to municipal liability in so-called "failure to properly train" cases, "deliberate indifference" by its police policymakers must be shown before a city can be held liable under Section 1983 for deprivation of rights. This standard of culpability is generally very difficult for plaintiffs to overcome.

Within the bystander context, the notion that any police officials, much less tactical unit supervisors and personnel, would choose a course or means for the delivery of force with deliberate and conscious disregard for the safety of innocent persons might initially seem incomprehensible. While one might more easily accept such a negative police attitude toward assailants and their constitutional rights, it would generally seem to be a far greater stretch for bystander-type plaintiffs to gain similar acceptance within the courts. The identity of the particular bystander could become relevant in this respect. Tactical unit supervisors can ill afford to ignore and should recognize any pos-

---

3. This tactic was recognized long ago and described by Sykes and Matza (1957) as a sociological phenomenon rather than a purely legal issue.

sible litigation fostering perception that they might be less concerned with the safety and constitutional protection of some bystanders than of others (*Africa v. City of Philadelphia*, 1994). Ultimately, however, just what constitutes deliberate indifference should in most instances turn on factors other than this perception. Rather, the most crucial inquiry will likely focus on whether or not police policies are adequate "in light of the tasks that the particular officers must perform within the usual and recurring situations with which they deal" (Bowser, 1986).

The threat of harm to bystanders inherent in the choice of lethal force is unfortunately a usual and recurring reality for the particular officers and supervisors within the tactical unit. Once again, foreseeability becomes critical in the legal analysis of tort liability because the tactical unit is specifically formed, trained, and arguably should likewise be armed to deal with extraordinarily dangerous events in a fashion that holds risk to bystanders to an absolute minimum. As has been asserted before, if the need for more or different approaches in the acquisition and use of advanced alternative weapons technology is deemed by a court to be so obvious and the inadequacy so likely to result in constitutional deprivation for bystanders, the usual shield to deliberate indifference may be imperfect.

While *O'Neal v. DeKalb County, Georgia* (1988), does not deal with a fact situation specifically involving tactical units, it serves as an example of litigation aimed specifically at requiring the police to employ less than deadly force and suggesting that failure to utilize alternative means of force is actionable. It, therefore, may be seen as generally applicable to tactical operations.

The survivors of a mentally disturbed man killed in a hospital shootout brought a Section 1983 action against county officials and the county, alleging deprivation of the decedent's Fourth and Fourteenth Amendment rights. The decedent went on a rampage through a hospital stabbing seven people in the process. Responding county officers, with their weapons raised, repeatedly ordered the decedent to drop his knife and lie on the floor. Instead of doing so, the decedent rushed toward the officers with his knife raised, at which point he was shot and killed. The United States District Court for the Northern District of Georgia granted summary judgment for the defendants.

The majority opinion of the Eleventh Circuit Court on appeal affirmed. It tested the officers' behavior under both the substantive due process standards of *Johnson v. Glick* (1973), and under the reasonableness of seizure standards of *Tennessee v. Garner* (1985). The majority held that there was no "conscience shocking" nor malicious behavior by the officers (the due process analysis), nor under all the circumstances could it be said that the officers' level of response was unreasonable.

However, there was a dissenting opinion in the case that is worthy of review. The evidence in the case included testimony from a police training "expert" who indicated that the officers had several alternatives available to them short of employing fatal force. The dissent enumerated and specifically identified up to six treaties that have been published in support of the use of less lethality, ultimately concluding that while there was no real dispute as to the facts of the incident, there was conflict as to the proportionality of the police force used. The dissent felt that a jury might find that the officers acted unreasonably in not pursuing alternative, less-drastic measures and that a constitutional deprivation actually resulted from the county's failure to train the officers in the use of such measures. By analogy a similar argument might be offered within the context of failure to provide officers with the types of equipment necessary to facilitate a so-called "proportional response." While this decedent is not of the innocent bystander variety, neither is he a classic criminal assailant. His type might thus be capable of invoking some level of favorable trial sentiment, particularly if the factfinder can be convinced that tactical experts should be held to higher standards of accountability than the police generalists that were involved in this individual case.

Langford v. Gates (1985) presents a fact situation directly involving degrees of police intrusion short of deadly force in the attempted search and seizure of both premises and persons. It also displays possible causes of action as might be raised by both assailants and bystanders under Section 1983 and state law as well.

The case challenged certain conduct of the Los Angeles Police Department as being in violation of the plaintiff's Fourth, Fifth, Ninth, and Fourteenth Amendment rights, and similar provisions of the California Constitution. The challenged practices were the use of an armored personnel carrier, equipped with a steel battering ram, to storm certain structures suspected of housing narcotics activity, together with the throwing of diversion devices through the holes created in the walls of the residences.

The "suspected" narcotics activity was verified by several buys. The structures had been heavily fortified by steel bars covering all windows and doors. In some cases the steel bars were both inside the windows as well as outside. The steel doors were backed up by fortified inner doors with steel bars imbedded in the concrete floors. The L.A.P.D. ram was never used on narcotics locations that were not so well fortified against the usual police practices for necessary forced entry.

The action was brought by five plaintiffs. Three alleged that they were merely "visitors in a friend's home" when the motorized battering ram and grenades were used. Included in the suit as defendants were individual officers, the chief of police, and the city. The case was the subject of proceedings in both federal and California state court systems with the California Supreme Court eventually engaging in an in-depth legal analysis of these practices within the body of its opinion. The essence of its holdings were that the use of pyrotechnic explosive devices could not be accounted constitutionally unreasonable and that the motorized battering ram could be used in executing searches only after police satisfied the following three preliminary requirements: (1) obtaining a warrant under probable cause, (2) receiving prior authorization to use the ram from a magistrate, and (3) at the time of the actual entry determining that there were exigent circumstances.

The so-called "rockhouses" that were targeted by the Los Angles Police Department are specifically fortified dwellings where rock cocaine is made and sold. Parallels to other forms of "barricaded subjects" (perhaps with hostages) that might be encountered by police tactical squads seem obvious.

The majority of the court took the position that the stun grenades or "flashbangs" did not pose an unacceptable threat to property and persons. The opinion noted in this regard that when "reduced to a proper level of explosive power, and used under agency guidelines requiring that detonation occur only after officers have seen fully into a targeted room, the devices carry a minimum risk of injury, certainly less than the use of guns to disarm hostile subjects" (*Langford v. Gates,* 1985). Also of importance in the court's view was statistical evidence that after a single fatal accident in 1984, the flash/sound device had been successfully used by the Los Angles Police Department in more than 25 instances while inflicting only momentary disorientation on suspects. Presumably the same desirable outcomes could be expected when the devices are properly employed to minimize risk to hostages or bystanders. Since *Langford,* flash/sound devices have been used by the Los Angeles SWAT Team more than 500 times with no similar injuries occurring.

The ram was a different matter according to the court. The risks from collapses of building walls and ceilings and rupture of utility lines, fire, and explosion constituted threats to owners, occupants, and neighbors that could be considered presumptively unreasonable unless authorized in advance by a neutral magistrate. Even thereafter, unless specific exigent circumstances develop at the time of entry, the court was in favor of less-intrusive tactics. A concurring and dissenting opinion written by the Chief Justice went to great lengths to identify factually some of the alternatives possibly available to the police in this type of case that would provide for less-intrusive seizures. On the other hand, one justice would not have required police to secure prior judicial review of this device and would simply apply an objective reasonableness test on a case-by-case basis considering the totality of such circumstances as the fortified nature of the premises; the existence of viable alternative entries; the expected resistance; and the risk of harm to entering officers, the suspects, and their neighbors.

In *Plakas v. Drinski* (1994), a Section 1983 action was brought against both an individual officer and his employer, Newton County, Indiana. The case involved the officer's shooting of Plakas, the deceased, during an attempt to arrest him. Plakas had charged toward the officer with a raised fire poker after unsuccessful verbal attempts to disarm him. Among other things, the Plaintiff as administrator of the deceased's estate, alleged that the officer was required to use all feasible alternatives before ultimately resorting to deadly force. While the court did specifically acknowledge three other options that conceivably could have been open to the officer (keeping distance between the officer and the suspect, using a disabling chemical spray, or using a dog), it declined to acknowledge any "precedent" which says that the Constitution requires law enforcement officers to use all feasible alternatives to avoid a situation where deadly force can justifiably be used.

Of more significance in resolution of any debate over appropriate arsenal alternatives for tactical units is a second holding of the court that there was likewise "in fact not a single precedent which holds that a governmental unit has a constitutional duty to supply particular forms of equipment to police officers." The court indeed quoted precedent to the contrary and ended with the policy assessment that it would be unwise indeed to "permit every jury in this type of case to hear expert testimony that an arrestee would have been uninjured if only the police had been able to use disabling gas or a capture net or a taser... and then decide that a municipality is liable because it failed to buy this equipment.... We think it clear that the Constitution does not enact a police administrator's equipment list" (*Salas v. Carpenter*, 1992).

Currently it would seem an uphill climb for plaintiffs seeking redress for police failure to use less-lethal munitions and the like particularly at the federal level. At the state level this effort may prove multijurisdictional with a wider range of adjudicative success. The use of diversionary devices is on the whole neither mandated nor prohibited by existing case law. However, a range of operational and administrative recommendations becomes obvious. First, it must be accepted that, even with the current state of the art being in a fledgling condition, technological innovations such as less-lethal munitions do possess a large measure of efficacy. They definitely produce the desired effect of temporarily immobilizing all parties to a hostage or barricaded suspect situation. They have also been shown to be effective as a preliminary to the execution of search and arrest warrants to neutralize the effectiveness of hostile and violent subjects and to prevent bystanders from moving in or into a crossfire zone.

Officer Safety Equipment

The original concept of body armor involved sewing overlapping strips of animal skin in a design much like a shingled roof into a vest-shaped garment. This device provided the wearer with limited protection to the torso over the vital organs from stones launched by slings. As the refinement of various metals became a reality, spears and arrows tipped with metal replaced stones. Accordingly, protection against this new form of weaponry came from metal sewn into the skin. As the ability to smelter and shape metal became more advanced, solid metal breastplates, chain mail, and helmets protected the warriors from the assaults of enemy spears, arrows, swords, and knives.

However, the armor was extremely heavy and cumbersome thus rendering the wearer into a relatively well-protected but immobile and vulnerable soldier. With the passage of time the armor became more decorative than functional to signify the allegiance, rank, and martial prowess of the wearer. As warfare entered into and emerged from the Dark Ages, body armor became a less important factor on the battlefield. Ceremonial uniforms were a greater priority than personal body armor until after World War I primarily because armor that could provide protection against bullets was much too heavy for the wearer to function and armor that was light and flexible simply did not stop bullets.

Thus, the specifications placed upon the armor industry were threefold: the material was to be lightweight enough to allow mobility under extremely stressful conditions, strong enough to withstand the penetration power of a high-powered bullet, and flexible enough to disperse the energy (momentum) of the projectile thereby reducing the severity of blunt trauma injury. A variety of natural and manmade fibers have been used throughout history in the construction of armor to achieve these characteristics. For example, silk was originally used in medieval Japan and in nineteenth century America. However, its ability to prevent penetration was limited to small caliber handguns. Experiments with nylon were conducted during World War II and the Korean Conflict. The protective vests developed with this synthetic fabric provided protection against many rifle bullets but were still too bulky and mobility limiting to warrant mass production and general issue to military troops.

Although a polymeric aromatic amide plastic fabric achieving the required characteristics was hypothesized as early as 1939, mass production was not possible until 1965 when DuPont scientist, Stephanie Kwolek, discovered a practical and economically feasible means of synthesizing polyaramid fiber. Marketed under the trade name Kevlar®, the material possessed a strength-to-weight ratio five times greater than steel for which it was to serve as a substitute in the production of radial tires. In 1971 Richard Davis joined several layers of Kevlar woven into a crisscross pattern to produce soft body armor. The resulting "bulletproof" vests were designed to accomplish the following goals:

1. The resulting material would prevent the projectile (bullet) from penetrating the body. Penetration can cause injury by tearing tissues, damaging and destroying organs, and causing bleeding.
2. The material of the armor would also deform the projectile thus widening it and slowing it and further decreasing the likelihood of penetration into the body.

3. Newtonian physics recognize that the momentum created by the velocity and mass of an object cannot be lost, only transferred. The weave and layering of the fabric would allow the garment to stretch without breaking to produce a lateral dissipation of energy.

The development of body armor made from Kevlar (R) and later Spectra® in 1985 provides tactical units with several distinct advantages:

1. Its relatively light weight allows the officer to wear the garment for extended periods of time even when worn with ceramic or steel inserts which dramatically increase the ability to defeat the penetration power of up to .30-06, 166 grain armor-piercing rifle bullets.
2. Its light weight also allows a large measure of mobility. This characteristic allows the tactical unit to perform the first two of its basic functions safely; that is, to control and contain a hostile situation. Mobility allows the tactical unit to add obstacles to the completion of criminal behavior and to remove the escape options of the criminal perpetrator.
3. The crisscross weave and layering provide considerably more bullet resistance than a comparable thickness of steel. This characteristic allows the tactical unit to take the steps necessary to de-escalate the situation without unusual risk to police personnel.

Although specific records have not been kept for tactical officers or other specialized police units, accounts maintained by the International Association of Chiefs of Police indicate that more than 2100 law enforcement officers have avoided injury and possible death by wearing body armor. Second Chance Body Armor, Inc. has accounted for 750 of these "saves" through its products alone. Thus, from a fiscal perspective, the cost of Threat Level IV protective vests (approximately $2000 per garment) for tactical personnel is inconsequential when compared to the medical expenses of even a single wounded officer and the social and legal costs of any inability to perform the requisite tasks.

Sensory Enhancing Technology*

One of the most critical needs in tactical operations is the development of information-gathering and data-analysis tools to improve

---

* Note: Material presented immediately hereafter with regard to varying forms of sensory enhancing technology as well as the subsequent commentary within this chapter on the relationship between surveillance technology and privacy rights and law is derived in part from: David B. Perkins and Tomas C. Mijares, "Domestic Law Enforcement's Use of Sensory-Enhancing Technology in Terrorist Situations," Chapter Nine of The Future of Terrorism: Violence in the New Millenium. Harvey W. Kushner (Ed.), pp. 173-182, copyright 1998 by Sage Publications, Inc. Reprinted by permission of Sage Publications, Inc.

response at scenes involving hostile, armed, and barricaded subjects. In most situations, unaided human senses are insufficient to locate and identify the subject and to determine the extent to which any criminal activities are being perpetrated. Besides the Texas Tower Incident, the 1985 confrontation between the Philadelphia Police Department and MOVE, the Ruby Ridge incident in 1992, and the entire Branch Davidian affair outside Waco, Texas, in 1993 are among the more recent and noteworthy examples of this principle where exceedingly accurate information regarding the exact location and activities about the barricaded subjects may have averted loss of life.

Although receiving less notoriety than these episodes, hundreds of incidents occur annually throughout the United States where there exists a series of common risk denominators. First, the criminal perpetrators actually caught in a tactical standoff not uncommonly possess the means, knowledge, and usually the motivation to use fatal force against the police, hostages, or bystanders who have found themselves in the line of fire. The ready availability of semi-automatic and fully automatic weapons, commercially produced and homemade explosives, and a tolerant, if not sympathetic following can transform a common criminal into a folk hero of mythic proportions.

Second, as previously pointed out, these incidents are law enforcement actions, not military operations. Unlike soldiers operating in the free-fire zones of conventional warfare, police officers are required to consider such factors as the presence of bystanders, local politics, instantaneous news media coverage, citizen complaints, and the fundamental standard that fatal force is an option to be exercised only on a conditional basis. Consequently, dependence on sheer firepower alone is insufficient. Firearms discipline must be maintained in all law enforcement situations and only that force which is reasonably necessary to the protection of human life is justified.

Third, once barricaded subjects are no longer in direct view, they can perform with cover and concealment. By keeping their own activities from direct observation, they can limit the tactical options of responding law enforcement personnel. Only with adaptations of various technologies can the human senses be improved enough to allow law enforcement responders to these situations to gather and analyze information, formulate a plan of action, and execute that plan while minimizing the risks to hostages, bystanders, other police personnel, and even to any criminal suspects.

The inability of responding officers to make informed tactical decisions is hampered because of human limitations to perceive many phenomena without some sort of technical assistance to intensify the senses. Several technologies have been developed to enhance the normal human ability to receive input from the environment before processing the data into useable information for making decisions. These technologies were originally developed for many different purposes but were later applied to law enforcement needs with varying levels of success, efficiency, and legal consequences. When modified by manufacturers and used by police tactical units, several technologies can provide important information regarding a subject's location, movement, and activities needed for the safe resolution of critical incidents involving armed and barricaded subjects.

Distance of Vision Reduction

ORIGINAL DEVELOPMENT. The most basic form of sensory-enhancing technology is based on the refraction of visible light waves. Through a combination of convex optical lenses originally conceived by della Porta in 1582 and later refined into a telescope by Galileo Galilei in 1609, the viewer is able to view distant objects and persons safely and undetected.

A much more intrusive form of surveillance equipment requires the user to drill a hole through the wall of a building to insert a plastic optical fiber. The tip of this fiber can be ground into a lens. The fiber itself, which is approximately the diameter of a refill tube for a ballpoint pen, can be fed to a camera and monitor from which the investigating officers can safely and surreptitiously view and record the activities inside.

TACTICAL APPLICATIONS. Since the ability to see is said to be the most profoundly accurate and reliable of the human senses, the applications become obvious. Countersnipers who are equipped with long-range telescopic lenses on their weapons are able to develop target acquisition much more accurately than personnel equipped with iron sights. In addition, they can use their telescopic equipment to serve as spotters for other police personnel.

ADVANTAGES: This technology is extremely affordable. Binoculars are available for under $50. Depending on the quality sought, night vision equipment is available in a price range from $750 to $3000. In some instances the technology can be modified for use on video and still cameras and can be varied for hands-free operation.

DISADVANTAGES. Whether using a simple pair of binoculars or a telescope, the user must have an unobstructed line of sight for effect. In addition, the distance usually results in an inability to hear any conversation or other sounds produced by the suspect. Finally, because this process causes a decrease in useable light at the eyepiece (ocular lens), telescopes and binoculars are of limited utility except during daylight hours.

Ambient Light Amplification

ORIGINAL DEVELOPMENT Infrared radiation is classified as the area on the electromagnetic spectrum between visible light (to humans) and microwaves (Laird, 1994). Infrared light was used by American military forces during World War II as an active device to identify the positions of enemy soldiers. It required a projector to bathe an area in infrared radiation which was invisible to the naked eye. The operator would wear special goggles with special lenses or could peer through a telescope with the appropriate filtration system to view the area "illuminated" by the infrared bath. Personnel within the area who were not using the special lenses would see only the darkness experienced in normal night activity.

Audio Amplification

ORIGINAL DEVELOPMENT. Sound is produced by the vibrations caused by the movement of an object. For example, human vocal chords produce sound when they are moved by the voluntary passage of air through the voice box. When an object vibrates, the surrounding environment (air, water, solid material) is caused to vibrate thus producing the medium in which the audible vibrations move. When the sound is too faint to be heard at a particular location by unaided human senses, various audio amplification devices have been used for assistance. These devices are relatively inexpensive ($50 for a stethoscope and $400 for the parabolic microphone seen at televised athletic events). Items such as contact microphones and probe microphones can cost $80 and $90, respectively, while electronic earphones which are capable of amplifying human voices from hundreds of feet away can cost $300.

Currently in the developmental stage is the laser reflector. As the name implies, this device directs a laser beam toward a window. Vibrations produced by conversations within the targeted room are trapped by the beam reflected from the window. The beam is reflected to a receiver unit where it is collected, and the vibrations are electronically separated from the beam. These vibrations are digitally converted into electronic impulses which are then reconverted into audible sound, thus reproducing any conversations conducted within the target room.

TACTICAL APPLICATIONS. Of particular concern to tactical personnel are the sounds produced by conversation and human movement. If accurately perceived and interpreted, these sounds can provide valuable information on such issues as the number of suspects and hostages, the activity and condition of these people, and by integrating these sounds with a voice stress analyzer, the anxiety level of the suspects, as well as those of any hostages, can be determined.

ADVANTAGES. The existing technology is reliable, affordable, and portable. It is easily operated and requires little training for operation and maintenance.

DISADVANTAGES. When sounds are heard through opaque walls, the actual activity may not necessarily be what was perceived. The laser reflector may ultimately result in the most accurate and useable information resulting in resolution of the problem. However, it is currently under development for mass consumption by law enforcement agencies. Its purchase price is expected to be relatively expensive.

Thermal Imagery

ORIGINAL DEVELOPMENT. Current thermal technology allows the observation of activities through a device (FLIR® or Forward Looking InfraRed) which has the ability to detect heat differentials from a distance and then translate the input into infrared images which then become visible on a video telescreen. Since unusual heat is often an indicator of trouble—either impending or immediate—the technology is used to monitor the condition of utility wires and circuit breakers, construction defects, motors and engines, furnaces and most other instances where heat is generated.

TACTICAL APPLICATIONS. This technology allows the user to make observations of criminal activity in crimes such as burglary and larceny where the cover of darkness is a tool for the perpetrator. As long as there is no surface to mask the heat emitted from the persons under surveillance, it can be used to detect the location and activities of suspects as well as the location, activities, and condition of any hostages. In addition to its use in observing criminal activity, its ability to detect heat through foliage allows this technology to be used for rescue work and to identify the location of decomposing bodies which are covered by as much as a foot of soil. It can detect the presence of humans who have been illegally crowded into freight cars during alien smuggling activities. Most recently the technology has been used to detect the "hot spots" in buildings and homes used for drug processing.

ADVANTAGES. This technology has been shown to be accurate and reliable. It allows inspection of areas and detection of activities not visible to the naked eye. Under many circumstances its use does not require a line of direct sight to be effective.

DISADVANTAGES. This technology is extremely expensive (approximately $30,000 for the simplest of units) and requires sophisticated training for proper use and continued maintenance.

Radar

ORIGINAL DEVELOPMENT. Radar (**Ra**dio **d**etection **a**nd **r**anging) is a technology using directed radio waves to observe the existence, distance, and heading of an object. Originally developed by Heinrich Hertz in 1886, the concept was advanced by a fellow German, Christian Huelsmeyer, as an anticollision device to detect ships and trains in the fog. Although its primary use has been to serve as a distant early warning system against airborne attack, it is also used commercially to aid in the navigation of aircraft and water vessels and to assist the military in the targeting of moving hostile ships, planes, and missiles. Radar technology has been used regularly in law enforcement to verify the speed of vehicular traffic.

The technology is based on the fact that electromagnetic radiation travels at a constant speed (186,000 miles per second) and that objects illuminated with a beam of electromagnetic radiation generally reflect and scatter that beam in all directions, including back to the source of that beam. By using a device known as a duplexer, the radiation may be alternately transmitted and its reflection may be received at the same point. The radiation can pass through a variety of surfaces and can be adjusted to reflect from only specific types of surfaces. It can operate under varying atmospheric conditions and does not need light to be effective. Thus, radar is not a line-of-sight technology and can be used in many situations where the exact location of the target or human subject is not visible.

TACTICAL APPLICATIONS. Low-range radar has been modified by engineers from the Advanced Electronics and Technology Division of Hughes Missile Systems Company to detect human motion through non-ferrous surfaces. It has been used in a law enforcement context under the product name of MDR-1® for search and rescue operations, for prolonged stakeouts, for locating barricaded subjects, and as an intruder alert.

ADVANTAGES. The MDR-1 actually allows law enforcement personnel to detect human motion through wall-penetrating radar technology. As a developed, field-tested, and marketed system, the technology is readily available and affordable ($5000 per unit). Approximately the size of a briefcase and weighing only ten pounds, it is easily portable. Since the signal processor restricts the sensitivity of the MDR-1 to motions from 0.5 to five feet per second, the normal range of motion that could be expected from a human being under most conditions is very realistic.

DISADVANTAGES. Although the technology is able to detect human motion through opaque surfaces such as structural walls, shrubbery, and trees, it is currently unable to detect the number of human subjects on the opposite side of the wall and it is unable to differentiate among the human subjects. Nor is it able to identify the activities or conditions of the subjects. Unless the surveillance personnel have employed at least three units simultaneously, the specific activities and the type and direction of the motion made by the perpetrators will remain unknown until verification from another source.

Resonance

SCIENTIFIC PRINCIPLES: Resonance is a phenomenon in which the vibrations, either natural or induced, taking place in one body cause vibrations of the same frequency in another body. Using a wide variety of applications primarily in the construction industry and in the medical field, this technology is able to detect sub-surface objects. The anomalous material beneath the surface will electronically produce its own distinctive "signature" which may be viewed either on an oscilloscope, video monitor, or graph.

TACTICAL APPLICATIONS. The principal tactical value of this technology lies in its ability to identify the types of materials used in a wall's construction. This type of information is critical when making a wall breach during an explosive entry. Water and sewage lines (either copper pipe or polyvinylchloride tubing signatures) would become a major inconvenience. Electrical lines (copper wire or aluminum conduit signatures) would necessitate a conservative approach. But, breaching a wall containing a natural gas conduit (iron pipe signature) would be a disaster. Using medical resonance equipment is neither affordable nor practical. Similar technology used within the construction industry is too inconvenient and too expensive for tactical applications. However, a relatively inexpensive, portable (approximately 2" x 3" x 6" weighing one pound) all-purpose sensor has been developed for use in the construction industry but is currently lacking the means for mass production (Marlowe, 1995).

ADVANTAGES. Once put into mass production, this technology would be very affordable (probably less than $100 per unit). It is extremely light and portable.

DISADVANTAGES. This technology is limited to only telling the user about the construction of a wall. The technology is currently unable to penetrate beyond the limits of the wall.

PRIVACY RIGHTS AND LAW

When the framers of the Constitution acted to guard against arbitrary surveillance over citizens, there existed relatively limited methods of intrusion into the areas protected by the Fourth Amendment. Modern surveillance technology poses a serious threat to individual privacy and freedom. While Orwell's book, *1984*, may have contemplated these technological realities, the framers could not have fathomed these risks (Pochurek, 1994).

A significant amount of literature has focused attention on the technology associated with electronic eavesdropping and the monitoring of electronic tracking devices (Scheurer, 1995). Cathode Ray Tube (CRT) microscopy (the ability to reproduce images "stolen" from a targeted computer monitor on screen without the knowledge of its rightful user) has also been reviewed (Rable, 1994). More recently, particular emphasis has been placed upon the increasing use of thermal surveillance by law enforcement officials in the war on drugs.

Some worthwhile parallels, both physical and particularly legal, may be drawn between this currently popular use of thermal surveillance, and use of the various forms of enhanced surveillance technology in tactical operations. More will be made of these parallels shortly, but it is appropriate that a more basic legal backdrop be introduced first.

Regardless of the nature of the surveillance devices discussed in the relevant case law, the landmark case almost always offered for analysis and application is the United States Supreme Court decision in *Katz v. United States* (1967). In *Katz* the Supreme Court provided the legal benchmarks for evaluating the American right to privacy by declaring first that the Fourth Amendment protects people, not places, and thereafter established a twofold test for courts to apply in individual cases. Put in the form of questions, this test asks first whether an individual has asserted a personal expectation of privacy under the facts, and second, does society recognize this expectation to be a reasonable one? Therefore, where a person either fails to assert or display a personal expectation of privacy, or where society under all the circumstances believes the claimed expectation is unreasonable, no Fourth Amendment violation occurs (Hale, 1995). What is really private and subject to reasonable protection has evolved within the courts into an extremely fact-specific inquiry, which the courts have approached under all of the circumstances of each individual case.

Further, the U.S. Supreme Court has recognized that an additional fundamental element for finding a violation of the Fourth Amendment is that the complainant must have a "justifiable interest in the privacy of the place intruded upon" (*United States v. Karo*, 1984). In reality this premise is just another way of saying that one who seeks to complain of the loss of a constitutional right must first have standing to do so. Unlike many drug interdiction cases, the prototypical tactical scenario is unlikely to present a situation in which the suspects will be found in a location where they have a justifiable interest in the privacy of the place where sensory enhancing surveillance will be utilized. While hostages may conceivably be taken in a location where they have such a privacy interest (e.g., their homes or offices), it is unlikely that they will complain of the police surveillance action on a constitutional basis. Indeed, a greater ultimate risk for the police relative to these victims may prove to be the failure to employ available surveillance technology (authors' emphasis added) if harm is caused to the hostages during rescue efforts. Even by modifying the facts to a point where a hostage taker or barricaded suspect is located in that most protected place, his or her own home, in most truly tactical situations the police are likely to already possess probable cause to believe that some crime has occurred. Thus, unlike drug interdiction cases, the warrantless use of enhanced technologies surveillance is not being used so much in aid of a search for evidence itself, but rather for officer, bystander, and victim safety.

Much has been made in legal commentary over the fact that the courts allowing the use of FLIR surveillance equipment in drug cases have focused attention on the means used rather than on the purpose for use and the resulting risks involved. Criticism is made that these courts refuse, by limitation of the term, to define FLIR intrusion as "searches" at all. Such a perspective, it is said, ignores a much broader interpretation of the term search, an interpretation that focuses on the true evidence-gathering motive of the police and the resultant invasion of privacy.

If indeed the motive, the essential purpose behind the police behavior is the appropriate standard for defining a search, as has been suggested by the critics of enhanced surveillance technology, then a necessary corollary argument would appear that the use of enhanced surveillance by tactical officers motivated solely by safety concerns is not in fact a "search" implicating the Fourth Amendment. Presumably, under this approach it is eventually the province of the court to discern through a totality of the circumstances and the specific evidence introduced in each case, what were the actual motives or purposes of the police surveillance.

There are other arguments that may be advanced in favor of enhanced surveillance in tactical situations. *Katz's* twofold test will in general not prove helpful to many barricaded suspects, hostage takers or terrorists in a complaint against police intrusion. Because of the settings in which these contacts with the police most often arise, the perpetrators will display no subjective expectations of privacy, nor would their expectations be deemed reasonable by society anyway. Indeed, high notoriety and publicity may be their expectations or even their desires.

Also, the whole field of "exigent circumstances" recognizes the balancing of individual freedoms and privacy interests against effective law enforcement and public safety. Under *United States v. Karo* (1984), in addition to addressing the issue of parties who possess standing to complain, the Unites States Supreme Court noted that exigent circumstances may allow intrusions that would under normal conditions be deemed intolerable. This position is consistent with the prevailing body of precedent handed down by both the high court and the lower courts when risk of armed violence is present (*Warden v. Hayden,* 1967).

There are, of course, possible cases in which tactical units may become engaged where the slight level of information available to them requires the use of enhanced surveillance not just for the sake of safety, but for the sake of additional information and evidence as well. For example, this situation may arise when the police have been contacted by a self-proclaimed but unknown terrorist or by an anonymous informant, and supplied minimal warning of an impending violent act which has potentially disastrous consequences. With only limited awareness of details as to the location, identity, armament, etc. of the perpetrators, additional corroborative evidence is required (*Illinois v. Gates,* 1983). Enhanced sensory surveillance devices might assist the police tactical unit in two ways. The devices may certainly provide information to help safeguard both the responding police personnel and the innocent bystanders in any subsequent arrest processes that occur. Even more, as an initial threshold to arrest, the information derived from these devices may likewise be corroborative evidence of the criminal activity itself. In this context, the use of such devices by tactical personnel can be seen as closely analogous to use such as in the drug interdiction cases. The substantive purposes behind their use are then at least in part a true search for evidence.

Conceivably, the surveillance might be of locations in which the alleged perpetrators or others who have standing to assert privacy interests, have taken steps indicating subjective expectations of privacy, and which expectations society is willing to recognize as being reasonable. Thus, the same issues addressed by the courts and critics of enhanced surveillance technology in the drug cases linger in certain fact-specific tactical events.

Even in so-called non-classic situations, responding police can (and no doubt will) continue to argue that exigent circumstances and risks to societal security justify the means. It has been said that "the doctrine of emergency in the law of search and seizure has never been defined in terms of its overall concept. The usual practice has been for a court to tailor its definition to the circumstances of each case." The preservation of human life may become the critical factor dispensing with the need for a warrant, for life is deemed to take priority over the right of privacy (Mascolo, 1992). Given the ever-increasing alarm of society over recurring incidents of both individual and mass violence, the courts may become increasingly prone to react with something akin to a "terrorist exception " to the Fourth Amendment's warrant requirement. Police use of ever-advanced sensory enhanced surveillance would seem likely to thrive should such an exception truly gain a foothold within the courts.

ALTERNATIVES TO CONVENTIONAL PURCHASING PROCEDURES

Irrespective of the type of budgetary mechanism employed by a law enforcement organization (zero-based, performance, program, line-item, etc.), the purchase process must follow four basic steps before the actual acquisition can be made:

1. Recognition of the need to acquire a particular piece of equipment either to improve the current delivery of police service or to replace existing obsolete or damaged equipment. This recognition should be a well-articulated statement identifying the item to be purchased, the price, source, and availability of the item, and the organizational ramifications; i.e., benefits of purchasing and consequences of failing to purchase. The overall needs analysis must be supported by empirical data and should not rely on emotional issues.

2. A public announcement of the intent to purchase and a request for bids. This announcement will describe the specifications of the item to be acquired and will indicate that, assuming that all bids will meet specifications and delivery expectations, the basis for selection will be determined by the lowest price among sealed bids which will be opened on a stipulated date.

3. Testing and evaluation of samples submitted from vendors to ascertain that specifications are met and to identify unacceptable samples. This phase should be conducted by personnel who not only will use the equipment but who also possess sufficient scientific background and can statistically and verbally explain their findings and conclusions.
4. Unsealing and opening of bids. For obvious political, ethical, and often legal reasons, this process should be conducted publicly.

Technological innovations, developments, and applications in all fields generally carry a substantial price. Whether the purchaser is law enforcement, the military, industry, or the general public, the price attached to any item must be carefully weighed against the benefits. Regardless of the purpose for the purchase (original issue, upgrade, or replacement), the acquisition process is usually characterized by a continuous conflict between fiscal managers and the personnel whose primary function is to fulfill the organization's goals and accomplish its primary mission (Iacocca, 1984).

Law enforcement's specific needs for technology and equipment are determined by the nature of current criminal activity. They are advanced from theory into action by the imagination and intellect of scientists, engineers, and scholars. However, meeting these needs is limited by the ability and willingness of many politicians to tax and by a corresponding reluctance to spend.

Sacrificing quantity for quality are both unacceptable options for the management of a tactical unit. Uniformity of equipment is essential for any team effort and the purchase of substandard equipment is not only a precursor to operational failure, it is also bad for organizational morale. For example, when purchasing a 37 millimeter projectile launcher, a rifled barrel may be slightly more expensive. However, it provides markedly improved accuracy over a smooth-bore launcher and thus reduces the chances of a tragic mishap.

Improvisation of equipment is a feasible approach only for the simplest of items such as mirror extenders, battering rams, and lights. Accordingly, realistic and workable alternatives to normal budgetary procedures must be explored, developed, and followed to increase the ability of tactical units to obtain this costly equipment.

Grants

One source of funding is through grants from the federal government and from some private foundations. Although not as common as during the period of the Omnibus Crime Control and Safe Streets Act of 1968, this source remains very popular for specific projects. Currently this funding method is primarily targeted for community policing and drug awareness programs.

Grant approvals are often dependent on a stipulation that once initially funded, these projects are generally financed by the "hard money" of tax revenues for continuation. In addition, their availability is too irregular to be considered a permanently continuous and reliable source of funding. However, they are too attractive to be discounted entirely and, particularly when sought in conjunction with a nearby university, they can be an excellent means of program initiation.[4]

Donations

Some departments have enjoyed great financial success from donations given through the generosity of private individuals, corporations, and civic groups. For example, much of the structural facilities and teaching equipment of the Los Angeles Police Department Training Academy were obtained through the gracious assistance of Jack Webb and Mark VII Enterprises. The Houston Police Department SWAT Team has obtained a mobile command post, sophisticated communications devices, surveillance and analysis instruments, and personal protection equipment worth a total of approximately one-half million dollars through the generosity of the Houston 100 Club. Compaq Computers, Hilton Hotels, Kent Electronics, Gallery Furniture Company, and Transco Intercontinental Gas Pipeline Corporation are some of the many businesses that have contributed significantly to underwrite some of the expenses for training exercises conducted by the Texas Tactical Police Officers Association.

With very minor exceptions these donations are unconditional gifts after the receiving agency has described the specifications and sources of the items to be obtained and left the actual purchase to the donor. This method allows the items to be obtained without the bureaucratic foot-dragging or commercial objections associated with the normal

---

4. Research and development units of many large police departments often employ personnel whose full-time assignment is to explore these funding sources. Many police departments of varying size have enjoyed a measure of financial success by working in conjunction with a department of criminal justice studies of a nearby university on this alternative funding mechanism.

low-bid process. For various political, legal, and operational reasons this alternative has not been exercised in every law enforcement jurisdiction.

Forfeiture

Under conditions of the Criminal Forfeiture Act (CFA) and similar state statutes, money and property forfeited by convicted perpetrators of organized crime activity may be used to assist local law enforcement agencies in further crime-fighting efforts. This process has been upheld by several court cases and is largely limited to assist in the purchase of equipment and in the continuing enforcement of organized crime enterprises, particularly illegal drug activity.

By name, the CFA may appear to be a contradiction in terms whereby civil procedures are used to obtain property acquired by organized crime figures during or immediately following their participation in criminal activity, particularly when no legitimate means of support is apparent. Current interpretations of the conditions needed for seizure require establishment of a connection between ownership of the assets to be seized and organized crime activity. However, because the property seizure is a civil procedure, only a preponderance of evidence is required. The amount seized by various law enforcement agencies since the CFA was enacted in 1984 is estimated to reach far into the billions of dollars with the majority of the funds disbursed to local police departments. Since tactical units often provide the uniformed presence during the execution of search and arrest warrants, some departments have used seized assets to provide the means to obtain the equipment necessary for continuation of this specific enforcement activity.

Excess Federal Equipment

In 1989 the 1208 Program enabled the Department of Defense to distribute excess[5] military equipment to law enforcement and corrections agencies with the stipulation that the equipment be used for drug

---

5. "Excess" refers to equipment that has been in stock for less than 21 days. After that time anything that has not been acquired or reserved by a federal, state, or municipal law enforcement agency is considered "surplus" and id made available, with fewer restrictions, to other agencies such as fire departments, schools, or hospitals.

enforcement action. Renamed the 1033 Program in 1996, the program was extended to all law enforcement activities with the understanding that priority would be given to drug enforcement and counterterrorism activities. With the variety in equipment almost unlimited, the following participation criteria were put into effect for law enforcement agencies:

1. The recipient must be a government agency whose primary function is the enforcement of the law and whose personnel are financially compensated and have the power of apprehension and arrest.
2. The property must be drawn from existing stocks of the Department of Defense.
3. Transfer costs are the responsibility of the recipient.
4. The recipient accepts the property on an "as is" basis.
5. The recipient must detail exactly how the property will be used and agree to use it within one year.
6. Property received cannot be sold, leased, rented, exchanged, bartered, or used to secure a loan or to supplement the recipient's budget.
7. All property transfers are conducted on a first-come/first-served basis.

Under conditions of the program, each state is required to have a governor-appointed coordinator to serve as a liaison between that state's law enforcement agencies and the Department of Defense. New excess property comes into the system on a daily basis and is catalogued and entered into a computerized retrieval system. It is the responsibility of the state coordinator's office to match requests from its law enforcement agencies with available property and to prepare the proper documentation accordingly. Using established channels of communication, interested tactical units should contact their state coordinator for participation details. Support and assistance is also available through the National Institute of Justice's National Law Enforcement and Cor-rections Technology Center.

Combining Resources

Typically, each member of a tactical unit may be outfitted with very sophisticated and expensive equipment. Depending on fabric selected, utility uniforms may range from approximately $75 to $ 400 per set. A similarly wide range exists for other individually assigned equipment such as handguns, automatic shoulder weapons, communications devices, ballistic helmets, body armor, footwear, gas masks, web gear, gloves, jackets, and balaclavas. However, since a SWAT team constitutes a relatively small part of a police department, equipment purchases tend to involve a small number of items to be purchased and discounts based on volume are unlikely.

Complicating the issue, expensive capital equipment such as sensory enhancing surveillance technology (radar, thermal imagers, night vision devices, audio amplifiers, etc.), specialized tactical vehicles (armored personnel carriers, mobile command posts, equipment vans, etc.), and weapons (tear gas, stun munitions, sniper rifles, etc.) tend to be used only on an extremely critical but usually infrequent basis. Thus, providing a rationale for purchase becomes a challenge when the tactical unit manager is usually questioned by an agency accountant.

A growing number of police agencies have found a large measure of success through lowering unit costs by buying for several agencies in a single purchase. Either through an informal understanding or through a formal contract these departments agree in advance to conduct testing and evaluation, submit a report to each participating agency, and purchase the item selected at a price greatly reduced from what would be available to individual tactical units. Similarly, some departments have found that sharing the larger, less-frequently used, and costly items described in the preceding paragraph requires each unit to spend only a fraction of what it would if making purchases independently.

PROJECTIONS OF FUTURE TACTICAL EQUIPMENT AND TECHNOLOGY

Police administrators must stay cognizant of the continuous developments in technology in all fields. Except for the advent of the automobile, law enforcement technology remained relatively unchanged over the previous century until the mid 1960s. Since evolution of the space exploration program, many products which had been developed for one field have been applied to many others including law enforcement. It can be reasonably assumed that these developments will continue and that there will be legal issues to be addressed with the associated application of these developments to the law enforcement field, particularly in those areas where the exigent circumstances of classical incidents involving barricaded suspects are absent.

Based on the past history and current state of technological development in tactical operations, a variety of conclusions can be made. First, it must be accepted that, even with the current technological state of the art being in a fledgling condition, devices such as less-lethal munitions and surveillance equipment do possess a large measure of efficacy. However, there is a potential for misuse and abuse and associated injuries. Consequently, at least until necessary safety and legal features are developed, these devices cannot be considered part of the personal arsenal of every police officer. Nonetheless, they can be employed by law enforcement personnel who have been specifically selected for this mission and trained by the equipment manufacturers and police instructors in the appropriate tactical use of these devices and proper safety procedures. These procedures, coupled with specific and enforced policies established by the law enforcement agency using these devices, must be followed as a first step to avoid allegations of police misconduct, particularly in the use of any technology involving the use of force.

Second, every attempt must be made to develop standards of the industry. The "standards of the industry" and "standards of care" expected of law enforcement SWAT teams will always change as technology provides improved equipment that can enhance positive resolution to violent events. Lights mounted on entry weapons such as pistols, submachine guns, and other shoulder weapons are now considered standards of the industry. Yet, many law enforcement agencies have not provided this type of essential equipment to their tactical units. Prior to 1974, light-mounted weapons did not exist in law enforcement. The first efforts were accomplished by police SWAT team members acting on their own initiative and ingenuity. Using available lights such as small standard flashlights and modifying pressure switches to the grips, stocks, and forearms of the weapons, officers improved their ability to see the threat, see their sights, and thereby fire more accurate rounds. The police equipment industry soon saw the demand for such equipment and manufactured continuously improved light systems for weapons.

Laser sights for weapons are another technical advance that have become a standard. Although more limited in application as a tactical tool, the laser sight is extremely useful in acquiring an accurate sight of the criminal suspect, thereby reducing the likelihood of collateral damage and injury to property or bystanders.[6] In addition, a laser can be used as a distraction or to encourage a suspect to surrender, especially when the red dot is displayed appropriately on the perpetrator's torso.

Less-lethal equipment has already been introduced into law enforcement in a variety of applications. Chemical agents have been a part of the law enforcement repertoire for decades, and over the years innovations from CN gas to CS gas and now OC (oleoresin capsicum) have been made. Improved, safer, and more accurate systems of delivery and application have created many opportunities for use by law enforcement.

Impact devices have moved from the old police "billy" club to 37 millimeter multishot systems with rifled barrels and sophisticated sights to ensure a much higher accuracy factor. These systems also fall under the heading of standards of the industry.

Police officers, sheriff's deputies, or federal agents are often confronted with violent situations where less-lethal tools are effective and appropriate. Torts may not necessarily occur solely because law enforcement tactical personnel are not provided with certain equipment (*Salas v. Carpenter*, 1992). However, the public outcry over perceived overreaction and the impact on community relations may be devastating if less-lethal approaches are not explored.

Thus far, sensory enhancing technologies have not been sufficiently accurate and reliable nor have they included the necessary redundancies to verify or expand upon the information obtained. At best the information can only provide an approximation of the necessary facts. Initially developed for medical, transportation, communication, construction, entertainment, and military purposes, these technologies can be modified to meet law enforcement needs. Since the signals received by these technologies are usually converted into electronic impulses, it is possible to integrate the impulses generated by audio amplification equipment, night vision equipment, radar, resonance, and thermal differentiation equipment and computer-enhance them into a virtual reality depiction of the situation in question, thereby providing the information necessary for proper decision making in response to the

---

6. Multiple laser sights on entry team situations are not advisable. Multiple red dots in a confined area tend to cause genuine confusionas to who "belongs" to each red dot.

threat posed by an armed, barricaded suspect. Informed decisions require details about the number, location, and reaction capabilities of the perpetrator(s); number, location, and condition of any hostage(s); and information about the physical layout of the premises not included in the construction blueprints.

Not only can this approach provide accurate information for immediate resolution of the problem of a barricaded suspect, it can also provide an audio and visual record of the activities taking place within the perimeter occupied by the perpetrator. This record could then be part of the evidence offered later for prosecution purposes.

Because of the potential for misuse of any kind of sensory enhancing technology, either through misfeasance or malfeasance, specific guidelines for proper use must be developed. Strict supervision must ensure that these guidelines are followed. Even when the users' actions are performed with the best of intentions, police administrators must proactively establish high standards for personnel selection and training in order to avoid the undue allegations of neglect that can occur.

Currently the database of incidents involving the use of technical advances is relatively small and may account in part for the lack of conclusiveness. To accomplish the development of standards, law enforcement agencies must become more willing to exchange information, particularly about relevant case histories. For several reasons, local police tactical units have been very reluctant to divulge information about their policies, procedures, personnel, and equipment procurement practices even with members of their own agencies.

In addition, organizations such as the National Tactical Officers Association, the International Association of Chiefs of Police, and the Department of Justice can and do serve as national clearinghouses of information. Even if adding to the current inventory of alternatives is not feasible or fiscally possible, the examination should be conducted in concert with a similar and continuous examination of case histories of actual tactical operations and any resulting litigation.

Finally, the police equipment industry must be encouraged to develop useable and close to foolproof innovations that will help accomplish the agency's mission without undue exposure to danger for police personnel, bystanders, hostages, and even the assailants. Currently, the largest inhibitor to the development of new and sophisticated equipment is the fact that law enforcement is a limited marketplace compared to the military or the general population. When police practitioners ask for newly developed technology or innovations, the first question from the manufacturers is, "How many will we sell?" Unfortunately, there are limited numbers of SWAT teams and most of them are hard pressed to purchase equipment because of fiscally conservative state, county, and city governments. This factor has been the largest stumbling block to the development of devices such as the rifled barrel 37 millimeter alternatives to the smooth-bore launchers of the same caliber on the market today.

The "phaser" weapons of the *Star Trek* television series may currently be only science fiction. However, experiments with nonintrusive weaponry such as sound pulses and focused microwaves are being conducted. Similarly, while the wireless hand-held communicators may have appeared as a fantasy for only a limited few, the cellular phones of today are smaller than and superior to the communication devices fictionally anticipated for the twenty-third century and appear to be almost universally employed. The move toward a technology that is capable of aiding tactical units in the fulfillment of their mission is an endeavor worth pursuit (Mijares and Perkins, 1995).

Chapter Seven

LEADERSHIP ISSUES IN
TACTICAL OPERATIONS

Managerial ability and leadership are critical in tactical operations for several reasons. First, for optimal success tactical operations require coordination of personnel, resources, and efforts. Coordination is both an internal and external managerial function that cannot and should not be relegated to subordinates. In order to adhere to the principle of chain of command when dealing with units outside the tactical team, an assertive and effective leader is necessary for the expeditious flow of information, the acquisition and transfer of material and personnel assets, and the prompt interchange of organizational stimuli (directives) and responses (reactions to orders). Second, management at all levels of the organization receives its authority from the organization, irrespective of the nature and strength of any relationship with subordinates. The organizational source of power is intended to facilitate management's attainment of organizational goals. Third, under the theory of vicarious civil liability described in Chapter Two, the organizational leader may be placed into a position of responsibility for the actions of subordinates.

Accordingly after defining some of the basic terms associated with management, supervision, and leadership, the following items will be addressed:

1. An identification of the roles played by persons placed into positions of responsibility within the organization.
2. An identification of the sources of power within organizations in general and a discussion of the relevance of these sources to the environment of tactical operations in particular.
3. A discussion of the criteria to be employed in the selection, training, and placement of supervisors in tactical assignments.

123

4. A discussion of the factors to be considered in tactical decision making.
5. A presentation of an historical tactical incident in which chain of command and leadership responsibilities are discussed.

BASIC TERMS

In the most general of terms, leadership can be defined as the ability to motivate others to do what they would normally not do to accomplish organizational goals. The need for organizational leadership is usually due to the unwillingness or inability of subordinates to take the appropriate action or, even more commonly, a lack of awareness about what must be accomplished.

Among tactical officers, motivation is usually not an issue. Because of the selectivity of assignment, the intensity of training, and the need for maintaining measures of knowledge, skills, and abilities at levels far above those displayed by most other police officers, personnel attracted to tactical operations tend to be naturally self-motivated. If anything, the energy and enthusiasm of tactical officers does not need prodding as much as restraint (Kraska and Kappeler, 1998) and channelling.

Inability to achieve organizational goals is usually due to a lack of preparation (training) or to inadequate assets (equipment, resources, and support). Training content and the learning process have already been addressed in Chapters Four and Five. As indicated, training and performance levels among tactical officers usually tend to exceed the measures attained by other police personnel. However, as part of the staffing function of management, it remains the duty of personnel in leadership positions to assess the training needs of the workforce continuously. This task requires a thorough understanding of organizational goals, knowledge of organizational resources, and an unremitting review of the strengths and limitations of organizational personnel. The task also requires the tactical manager to designate qualified training personnel and to implement the appropriate program to attain the desired performance levels.

Leadership through making subordinates aware of what must be done is a relatively straightforward operation in tactical operations. At the least this task involves keeping subordinates informed of the criminal activity needing the immediate attention of the tactical unit.

However, the more sophisticated units such as the Los Angeles SWAT Team maintain constant contact with the intelligence-gathering and analysis units of their agencies. In addition, continuous research is conducted by these organizations in the material area of long-term criminal trends as well as developments in the relevant tactics, technology, and techniques of law enforcement and the legal issues covering their use.

Although the task of keeping subordinates informed can be delegated, its managerial responsibility cannot. Too often the personnel in leadership positions develop a passive attitude toward this role by assuming that somehow the relevant information will automatically find its way to the tactical unit. If a tactical unit is to achieve operational success, management must assume a more active posture in this role and its members must not only be instructed and well drilled in the physical aspects of their assignments, they must be well informed about the overall environment in which their physical skills will be put to the test.

The "influence" exerted in a power relationship between supervisor and subordinate is defined as the effect of one party (the "agent") on another (the "target"). The outcome of any attempts to exercise influence can be seen as positions on a continuum. "Commitment" occurs when the target agrees with the goals of the agent and makes a sincere effort to carry out the agent's directives. "Compliance" takes place when the target is willing but apathetic and makes only a minimal effort to carry out these directives. When the target opposes and actively avoids carrying out the directive, resistance[1] takes place.

Influence can be exerted in an organization in a variety of ways. "Instrumental" compliance is the most basic of these processes and occurs when the agent controls the rewards and punishments of the system for either proper or improper behavior. Compliance through "internalization" takes place when the target supports the values of the agent. This process is usually a function of the agent's credibility, knowledge, and skill of communication. Compliance through "identification" is the most effective means of obedience because the target actually imitates the behavior of the agent through a form of admiration for the target.

---

1. Resistance is often construed as insubordination through actions such as making excuses, seeking a higher authority to overrule a directive, making delays, sabotage, and even refusing to carry out a directive. However, as long as the subordinate displays all due respect to the superior officer, it can be disastrous to demonstrate blind obedience when a directive is in violation of established policies and practices, contrary to published procedures, or even illegal.

ROLES OF LEADERSHIP IN THE SWAT ENVIRONMENT

Generally, leaders are important to organizations for several reasons that extend far beyond their specifically defined managerial and supervisory job descriptions (Bennis, 1989). Because a true leader personifies the organization and since the responsibility for the success of the organization rests with the leadership role, the true leader recognizes that the assigned position is not intended to be a reward for previous service but is a charge by the organization to perform new tasks at a level that invites vigilant public scrutiny. Depending on one's perspective, the blessing (or curse) of the leadership role is the increase of options available for problem resolution and the discretion to choose and use the appropriate option. To paraphrase a classic adage, "Success has a thousand fathers while failure is an orphan." Despite the realization that some form of criticism will follow almost any decision, the true leader assumes responsibility for the organization and its successes or failures as much as the authority to manage it. Because the tactical operation is such a high-profile aspect of a law enforcement agency, the SWAT team leadership can expect to be subjected to elevated levels of scrutiny and open criticism for any unit failure.

Organizational leaders have also assumed a greater importance than ever before because of influential factors outside the immediate environment of the organization. Because of massive and rapid developments in technology and because of the formal recognition of social diversity, today's society and its component organizations and institutions are characterized by continuous change. For example, the computer has given us the ability to obtain, store, and retrieve information with great speed, efficiency, accuracy, and capacity. However, the computer has also given hackers the ability to steal or alter information without detection. Criminal access to advances in technology has already been discussed and will be addressed again in the final chapter. Gender and multicultural considerations in contemporary American society have influenced what Samuel Walker (1999) describes as the most controversial issue in police employment, that of affirmative action. He notes that supporters believe it necessary to correct past discrimination while opponents argue reverse discrimination and the lowering of personnel standards. All the while, a confusing and inconsistent line of Supreme Court decisions on the subject add to assignment dilemmas (p. 312). The true leader not only serves as an anchor during these times of change and upheaval, but also provides the stability, insight, motivation, and wherewithal to provide guidance during all of these changes.

Finally, leaders are particularly important to public organizations because of a perception by the populace of the decay of values within time-honored institutions in our society. Dangerous liaisons and allegations of graft, corruption, and payoffs between special interest groups and government officials have produced high levels of cynicism. It is incumbent on the leaders of quality and class to reverse this trend and to execute their roles with dignity.

To cope with the importance associated with their positions, managers of tactical units, particularly those toward the top of the hierarchy, must assume roles that extend beyond their perfunctory duties of personnel supervision and organizational management. First, a tactical manager must serve as a liaison between the tactical unit and other units within the law enforcement agency. The role of liaison requires the manager (agent) to be an advocate, aggressively seeking assignments for periods when the tactical unit is not being deployed for "conventional" SWAT assignments. It also requires the agent to seek the material assets, personnel, and training opportunities needed to keep the unit at peak performance capacity.

A manager must also serve as a liaison with other tactical units in the overall law enforcement community. Counterterrorist units at the international level have often trained with each other and have repeatedly shared information on criminal suspects of mutual interest and on the most effective ways for neutralizing terrorist threats. The military structure of these units allows the time and resources needed to accomplish this task directly. However, domestic law enforcement agencies have little time or opportunity to train and share in a similar fashion because their normal, nontactical duties require their constant attention. Thus, leadership of the tactical unit must assume this responsibility to serve as a liaison and to disseminate the relevant information.

None of these roles can be accomplished unless the leader is also a tactician. This particular role implies that the agent not only possesses a scholarly grasp of tactics that is second to none in the organization, but also is able to convey that grasp both vertically and horizontally in an articulate, composed, complete, and concise manner at all times to

a variety of audiences ranging from the lowest ranking officer to elected political officials.

SOURCES OF LEADERSHIP POWER

Organizational leaders derive their power to direct the actions of
others through two primary sources of power (Yukl, 1998). Tactical
leaders are similar to leaders of any other organization in this regard.
As its name implies, **personal power** is the result of attributes possessed by the individual. These qualities may be based on factors such
as charisma, intelligence or expertise, connections (through personal
networking often based on friendships and loyalty). At its theoretical
extreme, personal power resulting from knowledge and skill is dependent on the substance of the skill and knowledge. In terms of practical
reality, it is necessary for the skill and knowledge to be valuable to the
organization. Equally important, the possessor must display these features in an inoffensive and nonthreatening manner, irrespective of the
type of skill and knowledge possessed.

Position power comes from the formal authority granted by the
organization. Acceptance of the leader's authority is largely a function
of the legitimacy of the organization. In the tactical context this condition requires official recognition of the existence, mission, and personnel of the specialized unit within the overall law enforcement
agency. Again the creation of *ad hoc* tactical units is not an effective
organizational response in terms of both legitimacy and efficacy.

Position power gives the leader control over rewards and resources.
This control entails more than compensation, but also progress,
assignments, work schedules, and tools for the completion of the
assigned task. While this power also implies control over punishments,
coercion or negative sanctions are relatively infrequent among specialized personnel because of the high level of motivation associated
with the selection process and rigorous training and because of the
high levels of performance needed for continued assignment. The
most powerful negative sanction that can be imposed is removal from
the specialized unit.

As indicated earlier, police personnel assigned to tactical units tend
to be highly motivated and enthusiastic about developing and main-

taining relevant skills and knowledge bases. People in leadership positions in the tactical unit should be no different. However, in any organization there are high-visibility positions that are often considered stepping stones to promotion and higher status levels and, thus, are greatly coveted. While merit, aptitude, attitude, expertise, and experience should be the bases for appointment to occupy these positions, subjective and arbitrary factors such as nepotism, favoritism, and politics have unfortunately long been within the domain of American policing (Walker, p. 24). Consequently, there is always a possibility that an individual can be placed into a position of leadership, responsibility, and authority with the attached position power without adequate preparation and development of a personal power basis.

CRITERIA FOR THE ASSIGNMENT OF TACTICAL SUPERVISORY PERSONNEL

Tactical supervisors should be selected on the basis of relevant criteria and not simply as a convenience for the organization. The latter basis assumes that all supervisors are not only equal but also expendable. They are also then viewed as being as interchangeable as replacement parts on an automobile. Stability is a primary concern in the assignment process. Placing a supervisor into a specialized position for building a career may be a relatively common move in some departments. The individual is placed into the position to allow a broad exposure to an assortment of assignments. This practice may benefit some individuals, but it does not allow sufficient time in the assignment to master the nuances of specialized assignment (such as SWAT supervision) and to improve the unit.

The corrupting influence of placing people into positions of leadership and responsibility on the basis of political contacts and allegiances to persons outside the organization was publicly recognized in 1937 in the Wickersham Commission Report (Bopp and Schultz, 1972). This system has not only been shown to lead to criminal corruption but has also been found to be too distracting for the individual to provide good leadership.

Instead of using outmoded, irrelevant, and ethically questionable criteria for the selection of tactical supervisors, these assignments should be made on the basis of personal attributes that will be employed in the management of every tactical operation.

Competence in this context comes from two factors. First, a supervisor should have a firm grasp of the substantive knowledge and an acceptable performance level of the skills of tactical operations. Ideally these skills will have already been developed through a previous assignment in the tactical unit at a lower level of the rank structure. The supervisor need not be the best shot with each weapon in the armory or the most skilled member of the unit, but should at least perform at a level to meet the minimum standards for continued assignment. Second, the tactical supervisor should possess demonstrated leadership and decision-making ability. These abilities are developed through progressively more demanding assignments in previous supervisory positions in organizational line functions. Skills and abilities developed through assignments in staff functions are generally not relevant or transferable to the tactical supervisor.

Courage means more than the willingness to confront an armed criminal adversary. It entails the fortitude, good sense, and discretion to advise politicians and agency executives when an operational decision made at the command level is tactically erroneous. However, the raw courage to speak out, even with all due respect, is meaningless and the resulting consequences of brave action could even be counterproductive unless consequences of directed action are identified and workable options are offered with practical and legal means and realistic descriptions to achieve these options.

Character implies that the supervisor is predictable and reliable in thought and deed and fair and equitable in the treatment of subordinates. While some people are concerned about doing things right, a supervisor of quality character is more concerned with doing the right thing. These factors of personality are developed through an acknowledgment of the organizational mission and a recognition of the individual roles played in that mission. A supervisor of quality character places self-interest subservient to mission success. When high-quality character in a supervisor is recognized by a subordinate, a symbiotic relationship is realized and many of the high-stress demands of assignment become automatic and willing responses.

FACTORS TO BE CONSIDERED IN TACTICAL DECISION MAKING

One of the most difficult of all leadership duties in law enforcement is to direct subordinate officers into a dangerous environment where the potential for injury or death is present. Tactical unit members understand the associated dangers and prepare for their mission with the clear appreciation that calculated risks are connected with the assigned tasks. The role of personnel in leadership positions in tactical units is to reduce the opportunities for continued criminal activity by the perpetrator and to increase the options available to the police.

This role can be greatly facilitated and enhanced first by providing relevant guidelines for behavior. These guidelines, established as policies and procedures[2] published throughout the agency, provide the general framework for action by identifying the goals of tactical operations (to contain, control, and de-escalate a hostile criminal situation) and by prioritizing the decision-making factors for achieving these goals. These priorities are based on the following order:

1. Lives of victims
2. Lives of innocent citizens caught in the area
3. Lives of law enforcement personnel
4. Lives of criminal suspects

In assessing these priorities the decision makers must consider the following questions:

1. Does the criminal suspect have hostages?
2. Does the suspect indicate in any way that the hostages will be harmed?
3. Does the suspect claim to possess the means to inflict this harm?
4. What sort of risks to innocent bystanders and residents of the area are presented by the suspect's actions?
5. What are the resources available to the responding law enforcement personnel?
6. What is the likelihood of any collateral damage by law enforcement personnel? (McCarthy, 1989).

One of the most critical elements of the decision-making process is timing, particularly during a hostage situation. The opportunity to

---

2. These policies and procedures, also known as "Standard Operating Procedures," "General Orders," and "Rules and Regulations," are characterized by their permanence and continuity within the organization until superseded by another permanent order.

neutralize a hostage-taker's ability to continue criminal activity may occur only once and usually without sufficient warnings for extended deliberation. Recall here that this dilemma was previously discussed in Chapter Two. The failure to make an informed decision may easily cost lives. One thing that is of paramount importance, however, is that the assessment of risks and the decision-making process must begin immediately because command personnel can easily be held accountable for unreasonable or excessive inaction as well as overreaction.

In a traditional barricaded suspect situation, the question often posed addresses the length of time that should be given to the suspect before physical means are taken to induce surrender. Agreement appears to be constant that all reasonable efforts should be extended to prompt voluntary submission to law enforcement authorities prior to the exercise of more aggressive action. However, there are differences of opinion regarding when the law enforcement response should be escalated.

On one hand there are those who believe that the mere passage of time will resolve these incidents and that a bond will develop between suspect and negotiator in a variation of the "Stockholm Syndrome" (Schlossberg, 1974). Proponents of this philosophy postulate that as the negotiation period extends longer and longer, the suspect becomes progressively more dependent on the negotiator for a resolution to the crisis and the negotiator, recognizing the signs of dependency, can heavily influence the behavior of the suspect to surrender or, at least, to act in ways that are safer for the responding police units. Under this approach, escalation of the continuum of force by law enforcement is entirely dependent on the criminal actions of the suspect.

The opposite school of thought argues that many suspects recognize the possibility of developing this bond and take the steps necessary to counter this police tactic. Extended waiting, particularly when no hostages are present, is interpreted as an opportunity for the suspect either to fortify a barricaded position, to develop countermeasures, to escalate the level of criminal force being used, or to develop the means for escape. Unless a quick response is initiated, there can be a demoralizing effect on the response unit and a debilitating effect on the community.

Both approaches have their inherent advantages and disadvantages. Rarely are there perfect tactical decisions for a simple resolution to very complex situations. Each approach and the many variations and permutations between them should be evaluated carefully by those in leadership positions along with the possible alternatives and likely outcomes.

CASE HISTORY: THE SPRINGLE STREET INCIDENT[3]

On October 17, 1988, at approximately 7:30 a.m., A man was observed by co-tenants of his Detroit, Michigan, apartment building carrying a gun and a can of gasoline through the building's hallways. A 911 call was made by one of the tenants shortly thereafter reporting the situation. The suspect, who had a history of mental disorders, was alleged to have harassed and threatened other tenants and was heard muttering to himself about a variety of disjointed topics.

A police patrol car with two officers in uniform from a nearby precinct was dispatched and arrived at the scene. The officers met the building manager who indicated that the suspect was in his apartment. Other residents advised the officers that the suspect appeared to be delusional and that he had accused several tenants of beating him and damaging his property.[4]

The officers approached the apartment and knocked on the door. The suspect responded by yelling obscenities and telling the officers to get away from the door. Despite continued efforts to persuade him to come out, the suspect refused to cooperate. One of the officers was able to push the door open a short distance and the suspect could be seen carrying a long gun of some sort. At this point the officers notified the dispatcher of a need for backup and a supervisor.

After assessing the scene personally, the responding sergeant verified that the subject was armed and acting irrationally. The sergeant notified the dispatcher that a barricaded gunman situation now existed and initiated building evacuation procedures. Pursuant to existing Detroit Police Department general orders, the precinct platoon

---

3. The description of this event is based on a review of the relevant portions of civil litigation resulting from the incident as well as the personal recollection of Tom Mijares who was serving as a sergeant with the Detroit Police Department at the time (*Walls v. City of Detroit et al.*, 1993).

4. The subject had accumulated serveral automobiles in varying states of disrepair and had chained them together on the street at the curbside directly in front of the apartment building. Earlier in the week Knowles was alleged to have beaten a man who had been sitting on the hood of one of the automobiles.

lieutenant and the patrol inspector responded to the scene. Upon their arrival they observed several officers evacuating the building and re-routing vehicular and pedestrian traffic. Likewise, pursuant to existing Department general orders, the patrol inspector, as highest ranking officer, assumed command of the situation and ordered all officers to don protective vests and to arm themselves with shotguns. The order to don vests was also directed to all police supervisors at the scene. The patrol inspector also requested the dispatcher to send a negotiator to the scene and to have the Fire Department and Emergency Medical Service available on a stand-by status. At this point approximately 45 minutes had elapsed.

For the next 45 minutes standard evacuation and containment pro-cedures were executed. At approximately 9:00 a.m., the precinct com-mander arrived at the scene, assumed command, and was briefed. Also, by this time a trained negotiator from the Tactical Services Section had engaged the suspect in a dialogue through the partially open door of the apartment. A safety chain kept the door from being opened further, but the negotiator could clearly see the suspect hold-ing a rifle, which he pointed downward while pacing back and forth. While maintaining his dialogue, the negotiator tried to open the door further by use of a prybar and a bolt cutter. The suspect requested that the chain not be cut and then unchained the door. The negotiator con-tinued to try to persuade the man to relinquish his weapon.

Several other officers were present in the hallway outside the apart-ment. Included in this group was the precinct lieutenant. Suddenly and without warning the lieutenant pushed past the negotiator in an apparent attempt to force the door. The suspect fired a single shot which struck the lieutenant in the upper left quadrant of his torso. The lieutenant was not wearing any sort of ballistic protection. After the lieutenant fell to the floor, the remaining officers removed him and carried him outside for emergency treatment. EMS personnel admin-istered to his wound, but since no ambulance unit was immediately available, the lieutenant was conveyed to a hospital in a patrol car.

Roughly twenty additional minutes elapsed, and at approximately 10:00 a.m. the Command Post was ordered to the scene. The Deputy Chief of the Criminal Investigation Bureau and the Executive Deputy Chief arrived at the location. As the new ranking officer, the Executive Deputy Chief relieved the Precinct Commander. He then designated the Deputy Chief of the Investigation Bureau as tactical commander.

Approximately one hour later the Special Response Team[5] (SRT) was ordered to report to the scene. After a brief "stand down" period, the team was deployed.

Based on intelligence about the suspect developed from a variety of relatives, neighborhood acquaintances, and medical personnel familiar with his psychological history, it was concluded that continued attempts to negotiate were futile and that conditions were not likely to improve with time. A crowd of onlookers and neighbors had also congregated and became disorderly and verbally abusive to the police officers. Further, school children had been dismissed from a nearby school and were attempting to return to their homes in the vicinity. The officers had been unable to verify if the suspect in fact possessed gasoline, but they felt certain that his rifle possessed the capability of penetrating walls and placing both police personnel and the public at risk. Collectively, this information reinforced the command decision to initiate an entry into the apartment. The tactical commander (Deputy Chief of Investigations) directed the SRT commanding officer (a lieutenant) to develop a plan.

The plan that was finally implemented called for CS tear gas projectiles to be fired through the windows from a 37 millimeter launcher. Additional gas would be thrown through a window by hand by an officer from a side window. SRT officers wearing ballistic Kevlar® vests with steel inserts and Kevlar™ helmets would enter the apartment after the gas had taken effect.

The operation was commenced shortly after 2:00 p.m. After the second of a proposed series of four tear gas projectiles was fired through a front window, the suspect replied by firing a rifle shot from the window. As the members of the entry team attempted to position themselves outside the apartment door, the suspect began firing through the wall, nearly striking them.

Believing that the gas was taking effect, the team proceeded. The point officer was utilizing a ballistic shield for protection and as a battering ram. After the door was forced open with the shield, the entry team sergeant threw a noise/flash device in an attempt to divert the

---

5. Although the Special Response Team was initially selected and trained in 1986, it had not yet been defined by the Department as an official entity. Consisting of three, five-person squads plus a nine-person command, training and support staff, each officer had been highly scrutinized for selection and received more than 640 hours of initial tactical training. Each officer had several years of police experience and most had been assigned to the Tactical Services Section or some other specialized line function of the Department.

suspect's attention. The team entered the room expecting to find the suspect in a location where he had last been seen by officers observing the situation from a nearby building. However, the suspect had moved to another position. This movement allowed him to surprise the team with an initial shot from his rifle, a shot which struck and fatally wounded the point officer. Remaining entry team officers then returned the suspect's fire, causing his death. Unfortunately, the point officer was not the only police death suffered. Despite an early rally, the previously wounded precinct lieutenant was eventually to succumb as well.

As might be expected, the deaths of the two officers raised postincident scrutiny of the event both externally and internally. In 1991 the personal representative of the estate of the deceased entry team officer filed a civil suit which included claims for wrongful death under Michigan state law and Section 1983 liability aimed at the City of Detroit, the Detroit Police Department, its police chief and deputy chiefs. With reference to the Section 1983 claim, the plaintiff alleged that the defendants were deliberately indifferent to the officer's safety by failing to follow Detroit Police policy and universally accepted police policy by not "waiting out" the barricaded gunman when lives were not in jeopardy. In ruling on the question of inadequate training, the United States Sixth Court of Appeals held that the deliberate indifference standard for liability in failure to train cases which was established by *City of Canton v. Harris* (1985) had not been satisfactorily proved by the plaintiff. According to the Court, the evidence in the case disclosed that the officers had received significant training (640 hours of initial tactical training for assignment to the Special Response Team). As for the issue of violation of its own policy and universally accepted strategy, the Court took notice of the department's written policy on barricaded suspects, but stated that even if the policy had arguably been violated, there were no conscience shocking orders present in the case. The Court concluded that whereas police work is recognized to be inherently dangerous, officers who voluntarily assume its risks possess no constitutional right to a reasonably safe working environment.

Whether or not certain portions of General Order 78-17[6] were factually violated by the actions followed at the Springle Street Incident

---

6. The text of General Order 78-17 was reproduced in its entirety and included as a footnote to the written opinion of the Sixth Circuit Court. Paraphrased in relevant part, it calls for a continuum of the tactical "escalation" as follows: (1) containment of the subject; (2) attempts to negotiate surrender; (3) possible introduction of tear gas to induce surrender; (4) assault when all else has failed and there is imminent danger of serious bodily injury or death to officers or citizens.

could be the subject of endless debate. Considering that the wording of the order, by first attempting the tactics of waiting and negotiating and thereafter forcing entry only upon concluding that a continued standoff threatened lives, it can be asserted that departmental policy (the general order) was in fact substantively followed. Therefore, it would be similarly arguable that the real issue in the case under either departmental policy or "universally accepted practice" analysis was not a simple matter of whether waiting/negotiating is generally preferable to entry. The real issue was (and is) at what exact time and under what exact circumstances does one make the choice to alter the initial tactics. In short, at what point does the risk of further delay become imminently life-threatening? Completely unanimous agreement is unlikely to ever exist here, and the decision to "move in" will inevitably be second-guessed by someone, perhaps even fellow officers, if there are casualties.

However, an even more primary question may be that of just which police responder gets to make the tough call to escalate from negotiation to the use of force, regardless of the rank held by that officer? General Order 78-17 may serve as a useful example for closer scrutiny of this question as well as other management and command structure issues.

The order was published by the Detroit Police Department approximately ten years prior to the incident. However, it had been in effect in one form or another for several years. It had been changed periodically, primarily to account for departmental reorganization that had occurred which included new rank structures and nomenclature within the chain of command. During the ten-year period following its publication, the field of tactical operations had evolved in several ways, including recognition of variations in the nature, motivations, and techniques of criminal behavior, as well as variations in the SWAT response. Collectively the evolution also resulted in increased recognition that a singular "pat" approach to resolution of a barricaded suspect situation might not be the best strategy. Also, there was a dawning trend of thinking that in episodes requiring SWAT involvement, chains of command and their related cumbersome orders of ascension and communication should be shortened and thereby simplified. In this particular incident, while consistent with the department's then-existing policy, a number of different individuals were in charge of the scene at one time or another, each requiring a complete briefing of the situation.

Utilization of a lengthy chain of command also assumes that all command personnel and supervisors are equally able to perform the duties associated with these situations. In actuality, when there is no continuity of leadership, each leader who becomes engaged brings a different bank of experiences, expertise and perspectives to the scene. At certain times under such a system there may exist a tendency toward micromanagement on the part of the command staff because of a lack of familiarity with the capabilities or limitations of SWAT personnel. Because of the amount of time needed to perform the usual functions associated with higher rank, there are often limits on the ability for these senior officers to stay apprised of the newest developments in the field. If taken to an extreme, a tactical event could assume the look of an undesirable *ad hoc* performance. Coincidentally, direct involvement in taking command of a situation may also "effectively negate a negotiator's strategy of stalling for time by referring the offender's requests and demands to a higher authority" (Wargo, 1989). If nothing else, direct engagement of an agency executive not familiar with the nuances of SWAT operations may be a distraction to the functioning officers.

Shortening the chain of command recognizes and is based upon the assumption that the tactical unit supervisors are the truer specialists in the safe and legal de-escalation of hostilities and assessors of the appropriate time and circumstances in which to modify tactics. This assumption is based upon their own specialized training and direct awareness of the capabilities, strengths and weaknesses of their units and the officers' strategic position relative to that of the perpetrator. This situation is analogous to the conduct of personnel at any other crime scene, such as a homicide investigation, wherein the detective in charge is recognized to be in complete control of the case including possessing the authority to determine who may and may not enter the crime scene (regardless of rank), what sort of evidence should be obtained, and what sort of techniques should be employed to obtain a successful conclusion to the investigation. Executive personnel should merely be apprised of any changes in the situation and, under the concept of *management by exception*, would become involved only if more "general" agency policies become violated.

Chapter Eight

INCIDENT MANAGEMENT

The success of the SWAT concept nationwide is impressive. Each week of each year multiple incidents of armed suspects, some holding hostages, are resolved successfully. Notwithstanding these success stories, not uncommonly the incidents that receive heavy media attention are those incidents with outcomes that bring the law enforcement agency criticism. However, incident commanders should not have concerns about overreaction or poor performance if their agency SWAT team is at pace with contemporary standards throughout the United States. If the incident commander does not know the team's capabilities, this would indicate the agency is not well prepared to respond to a critical incident requiring deployment of the SWAT team.

Once a SWAT team has been made into an operational unit of the law enforcement agency, the actual management and ultimate resolution of a critical incident requires various proactive measures to be taken by the organization. The purpose of this chapter is to identify certain organizational issues that must be addressed after creation and training of the unit has occurred, but which arise either prior to or during an incident.

ACTIVATION AND MOBILIZATION PROCEDURES

Mobilization that is tailored to the critical incident is crucial to a professional response. An approaching fire or a potential dam break or an approaching storm allows for extensive placement of all Incident Command System (ICS) components. A deranged gunman rampaging through a crowded shopping mall requires immediate tactical response.

Law enforcement organizations must have a workable and practical emergency response process that is tailored to their agencies and capabilities. The emergencies that require a SWAT response are not always obvious to first responders. Often a citizen will report a suspicious person to the police. This type of call will elicit only one patrol officer to provide initial investigation and assessment. The call may end with no police action required other than the single patrol officer's response or the call may become the community's worst nightmare.

There is, at times, a reluctance to activate a significant police response because of the fear of being accused of overreaction. The Springle Street Incident, described in Chapter Seven, can be instructive here. An obviously unstable man with a rifle had come to the attention of the police department at approximately 7:45 a.m. Two hours later a police lieutenant was shot by the suspect. At 10:00 a.m. the command post was ordered to the scene. One hour later a directive to mobilize the Special Response (SWAT) Team was finally given. The question is thus raised as to the appropriate time frame for actual deployment of a SWAT team. Why should there be any delay in the SWAT team being deployed when a man with a gun has shot a police officer and barricaded himself to avoid arrest?

The activation of a SWAT response does not mean that deactivation is not possible at any juncture when circumstances dictate a reduction in the deployment of agency assets. There are several examples of violent suspects expanding the threat to the community and to the police officers in the area precisely because SWAT officers were not available or deployed. The North Hollywood Bank of America Shootout is representative of how quickly a violent incident may end with interdiction by tactical officers.

The mobilization of SWAT and other department resources must be well conceived and tailored to the problem. This process should not be driven by a fear of accusations of overreaction or a concern about paid overtime or other less-critical concerns than citizen safety. The old cliche, "Better to be safe than sorry" can easily apply here.

A patrol sergeant should be free to mobilize a SWAT team based upon the sergeant's trained evaluation of the problem. And, under especially unique emergency circumstances, such as the North Hollywood incident, even patrol officers should be authorized to activate a

SWAT response. Accordingly, recruit training and regularly scheduled in-service patrol training programs should direct at least some attention to an understanding of the SWAT concept and should include instruction in the recognition of the developmental signs of a critical incident. Furthermore, semiannual training scenarios that allow for the agency to collectively practice mobilization and reaction to a variety of critical incidents are recommended.

The authority to activate a SWAT unit varies among police departments around the United States. The usual procedure begins with a patrol officer or a patrol supervisor realizing the need for tactical assistance at a crisis situation. Assistance is requested through a dispatcher who forwards the request through the appropriate chain of command. In some agencies approval for activation is immediate with department policy acknowledging the experience, training, insight, and overall abilities of the patrol supervisor to recognize the imminence of a crisis and the immediate need for a tactical response. In other agencies the mobilization calls for a step-by-step approval at each link of the chain of command. The rationale for a more detailed approach is based on the need for executives of a major subdivision of an agency to be informed personally of any activity and movement of personnel and other assets under their command and for the commanders of geographical areas (precincts, districts, wards, etc.) to retain control of any situation within that territory. This latter approach is generally felt to be outdated and may become a contributing factor to some tactical failures.

As previously noted, experience now suggests that one of the single most important components of critical incident command is a short chain of command. Therefore, specialized tactical units relatively close to the center of the organizational hierarchical chart appear to function more efficiently and expeditiously, particularly during the early stages of a critical incident (Thompson, 1988). Once again, the most significant aspect of that short chain of command is the delegation of the numerous responsibilities downward from the incident commander to those who are specifically trained and prepared to resolve the emergency. Incident commanders are often less than thoroughly trained and experienced in function and application of the SWAT team possessed as a tactical resource. They often do not know the precise duties and actual abilities of the unit's individual members. This lack of knowledge leads to uncertainty and even fear of using the SWAT team when it is the only reasonable solution. The insecurity that an incident commander may have is the strongest argument for the delegation of tactical activities to the SWAT commander.

Historically, such delegation has been difficult for some command personnel. During the early days of scientific police management there was an assumption that all command personnel could develop the capability to oversee any critical incident. Surrender of authority and responsibility to a specialized unit was considered to be an affront to one's management capabilities. However, because of the complexity of many current critical incidents, surrender and delegation of authority should not be viewed as professionally threatening.

The delegation is done with ease when the situation is an explosive device. The Bomb Squad is immediately notified. Upon arrival at the scene, the unit's command structure is given absolute control over the mission of neutralizing the bomb. All of the on-scene entities provide any and all support and backup, primarily in the form of keeping citizens and nonessential personnel away from interfering with the safe completion of the mission.

The SWAT commander should similarly be able to make a rapid evaluation of the tactical problem and quickly delegate to team supervisors the various options that can be employed for a response. The first concern of the SWAT commander is to provide a response capability as soon as possible. It may never be necessary to actually initiate a tactical response. The exact response would be predicated by the actions of the criminal suspect. However, the tactical commander, who has received extensive training in these matters, should be able to put a response into operation when necessary.

During the fledgling days of tactical units notification of individual team members to mobilize and assemble for a tactical response was somewhat time-consuming especially in the departments where SWAT assignments were made on a secondary and part-time basis. A general broadcast on the police radio to assemble at a designated location would be made for on-duty personnel. For off-duty personnel and officers assigned to investigative and administrative functions, individual telephone calls would be made. Today with the availability of individually assigned pagers, unit notification is a simple and swift matter.

RESOURCE ALLOCATION

There are numerous small and large-agency SWAT teams in the United States that are understaffed. Most police departments are understaffed but must find a way to function under the limitations of small budgets and lack of personnel. For years mutual aid has been the solution to the relatively infrequent but large and unusual occurrences that happen in small jurisdictions. So, too, should SWAT teams seek outside support when it is apparent that the violent incident or suspects being confronted require more SWAT officer positions than the host agency can afford.

Many large departments, some with seven hundred to one thousand officers, have full-time SWAT teams. Any agency that is large enough to require seven hundred or more sworn personnel should staff a SWAT team that is tailored to the size of the community, its population, the overall crime rate, the suicide rate, and the number of risk institutions that exist within the jurisdiction. Certainly court buildings, prisons, jails, and halfway houses are typical of risk situations and locations where violence can occur.

Based on current staffing formulae and operations of cities of comparable size, a city with a population of three hundred thousand or more would require a SWAT team of twenty to thirty-two members or more. When SWAT teams consist of these numbers, there is no suggestion that there are that many officers immediately on duty when an emergency strikes. Should a violent incident occur during prime vacation months, approximately one-fourth of the officers will be on vacation. Other factors such as illness, injury, normal leave days, or rotating shift assignments can reduce the number of available officers even more.

Whether the situation involves an armed robbery in a corner market, a mentally deranged suspect shooting up a neighborhood, or a distraught father holding his children hostage and threatening to kill them after he has killed his wife, the minimum number of SWAT personnel that should respond to a "typical" incident can easily be determined. Any of the above scenarios could occur in any geographic area and would require containment on all four sides. The general guideline suggests responding personnel to be assigned in teams of two for containment positions. Thus, merely containing the situation requires a minimum of eight officers. Personnel assigned as marksmen are held to a minimum and are usually positioned at exit points, usually at the front and rear of the location. Five more officers are needed to staff an arrest, entry, and reaction team. The response would also require the presence of a SWAT supervisor, usually a sergeant, and the SWAT commander, usually a lieutenant or above. The SWAT commander serves as a liaison between the overall incident commander and the SWAT team while the SWAT supervisor is responsible for the performance of the individual team members.

Some operations can be accomplished with fewer officers. Other operations can require more SWAT personnel. For example, a situation involving hostages could continue for several days and relief personnel would be needed. If a situation becomes mobile, several officers would be needed for a vehicle assault.

Whenever a SWAT position is eliminated, for whatever reason, the potential for failure increases dramatically. Suspects confronted in these situations are not entirely predictable and situations are usually in a state of flux, requiring adjustment, flexibility, and a wide range of options among responding personnel. As police personnel are removed from the situation, the range of options is decreased. The mission of the SWAT team is to contain, control, and de-escalate a volatile situation without depleting the overall organization's ability to respond to other, more routine, calls for police service. If decreasing the SWAT response is carried to an extreme, law enforcement management's options are reduced to allowing continuation of criminal activity by the perpetrator or moving to the final point of the continuum of force options; that is, the exercise of fatal force without any sort of graduated response from the lower end of the continuum.

When an incident has a negative outcome, the media, special interest groups, and the community immediately begin to focus on the shortcomings of the police department. Having too many options has never been an issue. However, there is a long list of failures where insufficient numbers of trained and coordinated personnel led to the loss of life.

COMMUNICATIONS

All critical incidents, whether they involve a barricaded suspect with hostages, a riot, a dignitary protection operation, or any other of the activities that require teamwork and coordination should have access to radio equipment dedicated specifically to that purpose. An experienced dispatcher should be assigned to relay and transmit all communications activity and to provide any resources and services needed for the resolution of the incidents. Preferably the dispatcher assigned to this duty is well experienced in communications operations and has trained for this specific type of assignment with supervised practice.

A specific radio frequency should be dedicated solely for use in the coordination of the incident and should be made available to all personnel associated with its safe resolution. Under no conditions should personnel not directly assigned to the incident use the dedicated radio frequency for unrelated communications traffic. Strict policies and procedures regulating the proper use of this departmental resource should be published and put into effect.

The dispatcher should be thoroughly briefed about the incident by someone with first-hand information about the sequence of events and the current status of the situation. Ideally the dispatcher should have access to a drawing, map, or other schematic depiction describing the geographical and physical characteristics of the area of the operation. Today's era of cellular fax machines and other information-relaying equipment makes this task relatively easy.

Personnel assigned to the inner perimeter as an entry team should have access to a radio system with the following characteristics: (1) It should allow hands-free operation with voice activation either from a throat or an ear microphone. SWAT personnel often wear gloves and carry multiple weapons and ballistic shields. They should not be concerned with fumbling for a transmission key especially when under the levels of physical and psychological stress inherent in these situations. (2) It should allow reception through individually assigned earphones to prevent criminal suspects from overhearing the approach of the entry team. The audio warning given to the barricaded suspect from radio speakers of one of the nearby supervisory officers was a definite factor during the Springle Street Incident described in Chapter Seven.

RELATIONS WITH OTHER AGENCIES

Police agencies with small resources in terms of tactical equipment and personnel have found great success through their participation in either of the two different styles of mutual assistance pacts described in Chapter Two, especially when joined by a large department and its greater tactical resources. Even the larger departments are well served at least to investigate the feasibility of participating in these pre-incident arrangements. Although relatively infrequent, there is always a possibility that a large city could experience a situation that is beyond its ability to manage.

During the initial stages of the Branch Davidian Incident, members of the local police department were dispatched to the city hospitals to provide security at these locations. The first teams from other cities to arrive had traveled approximately 100 miles and were from the Austin Police Department and the Travis County Sheriff's Office. They immediately began procedures to reinforce the federal officers from the Bureau of Alcohol, Tobacco, and Firearms (ATF) and to control and contain the activities of the cult members. Meanwhile, SWAT teams from Dallas (125 miles away), Houston (150 miles away), and the Texas Department of Public Safety formed an outer perimeter. This coordination of effort by local agencies who had traveled several miles was enhanced by the fact that they had frequently trained together at scheduled joint training sessions sponsored by the Texas Tactical Police Officers Association.

In addition to preparatory arrangements with other law enforcement agencies, agreements for assistance should be made with other local public safety departments such as the fire department and the emergency medical service. These agreements should be embellished by joint training and practice sessions.

Similar arrangements should be made with public utility companies in the event that natural gas, electrical, water, and telephone service may be affected. Coordination and cooperation may also be needed with the public transportation industry and related regulatory commissions if the criminal perpetrators attempt to become mobile.

REHEARSAL

The old adage that "Practice makes perfect" has a direct application to tactical operations. Not every incident allows sufficient opportunity for a rehearsal and not every rehearsal can replicate situational conditions exactly. Once again, North Hollywood comes to mind. Viewed as the logical extension of training, there are several benefits to conducting a rehearsal as often as possible.

First, a rehearsal allows supervisory personnel to observe a simulated performance, thereby identifying any need for further police assets, either in the form of personnel or equipment. Reinforcements and extra equipment are easier to find and put into operation during a rehearsal than after a crisis has escalated uncontrollably.

Second, a rehearsal can identify potential problems, particularly if the physical conditions can be replicated. While a schematic description is very helpful, a "hands-on" experience is priceless. For example, specific knowledge about how a door opens is helpful. Experiential familiarity with its physical characteristics such as friction resistance and noise can be invaluable.

Third, rehearsal provides information about the anticipated chronology and amount of time between the events of a crisis. This information is critical when the actions of one aspect of the operation are dependent on the amount of time needed to complete another aspect. For example, a distraction device may be employed during a hostage rescue operation and followed at a designated time by an entry from a different location.

Finally, just as an athletic team becomes more efficient and proficient as it repeatedly runs a play during a practice session before a game, a SWAT team removes superfluous movements with a rehearsal. Excessive movements, both individual and collective, can easily alert the criminal suspect to the approach of rescue forces and thereby jeopardize the safety of any hostages and compromise the completion of the mission.

EXECUTION OF PLANS

Throughout the execution of the plans it is necessary for management to evaluate the situation continuously and to be aware of the dynamics of the crisis. While some crises have relatively predictable patterns and almost appear to be scripted, the types of crisis situations involving a police tactical response are generally highly charged with emotions and subject to the almost whimsical and occasionally capricious nature of human behavior. Because of the extreme variations of response to similar provocation and catalysts, even the most familiar of surroundings and circumstances can produce very different results. Thus, it is vitally important for management to monitor and evaluate each stage and change in the operation, preferably with the input of a trained behavioral science expert with experience in law enforcement.

In addition, the operation should not be regarded as a competition between the criminal suspect and law enforcement personnel nor should it be allowed to degenerate into a battle between egos. Often the criminal suspect actually may have a desire for the crisis to be de-escalated, but has an even greater desire to "save face" and to be perceived, at least in his own mind, as a "winner." As long as the suspect can be arrested with a minimum of force, the police are in a position to discount personal issues easily and do whatever is necessary for resolution. The tactical mission continues to be the safe resolution of the crisis. Thus, it may be necessary for any invitation for the criminal suspect to surrender to be worded in a nonthreatening, nonconfrontational, and nonembarrassing manner. Any approach intended to lower the suspect's anxiety level and provide a means for a peaceful surrender should be pursued.

As long as it can be done safely, every effort should be made to record the operation electronically. This approach has distinct benefits that have been experienced through the use of video cameras mounted on patrol cars. First, it can provide evidence to be used in criminal proceedings against the suspect. Second, hopefully police officers always perform their duties professionally, but when law enforcement personnel realize that they are being recorded, they experience a variation of the "Hawthorne Effect"[1] and their performance and demeanor tend to improve markedly. Third, the recordings can be extremely valuable when responding to the fraudulent allegations of police misconduct. Finally, each tactical operation can be a learning experience regardless of the outcome. The educational benefits of these recordings are obvious.

---

1. During a study of physical working conditions in 1921, researchers found that productivity improved when members of the labor force realized that management actually displayed an interest in their well-being. Instead of emphasizing physical or technological variables, the researchers concluded that social and psychological factors were more important when studying worker productivity (Stojkovic, Kalinich, and Klofas, 1998).

POSTINCIDENT CRITIQUE

A critique is a supervisory evaluation of the event and should include six specific elements. The critique does not take the place of any criminal investigation report or other official law enforcement or prosecutorial document. In this context it is intended to evaluate the efficacy and efficiency of actions taken by tactical personnel.

1. The analysis should begin with a chronological summary of the sequence of events including the information leading to the request for police intervention and the means by which the request was made. Any history of similar police encounters with the criminal suspects should be incorporated with this section along with a disposition of each encounter. Any arrested perpetrators and the criminal charges brought against them should be noted. Actions taken by tactical personnel should be described in the summary of events. This description should include reference to designated assignments, activities of the criminal suspect that precipitated any subsequent law enforcement reaction, and the outcome of these police reactions.

2. Observations made by any witnesses, whether supportive or hostile, should be summarized. Verifiable addresses and telephone numbers should be included in the event that follow-up interviews are necessary for clarification or corroboration.

3. Physical evidence and its disposition should be described. This section should also identify the owners of any items seized. In recognition of the importance of a strict chain of evidence and the legal consequences for its violation, the location of its storage and the corresponding evidence inventory catalog number should be recorded.

4. The basis for the evaluation extends to more than the safe resolution of the crisis and the neutralization of the perpetrator's ability to continue criminal activity. The status of any prosecution should also be described. Similarly, the supervisory officer should indicate if the actions taken were consistent with existing department policies and established procedures. As indicated earlier, policy should be in accord with existing legislation, current case law, and standards of the law enforcement profession.

5. Since the document is an evaluation, the supervisor should make a recommendation regarding the need for any further action. If the supervisor's evaluation indicates that the actions taken were appropri-

ate and that the crisis was properly resolved, the matter should be closed pending any criminal prosecution of the perpetrator and the incident should be recorded for use as a training scenario. More importantly, if the actions taken were above and beyond expectations, a recommendation for recognition of meritorious service should be made and publicly acknowledged. Conversely, if the actions of any personnel reflect departures from policy or if the policy requires reevaluation or modification, a suitable level of corrective action should be initiated at either the individual or organizational level.

6. Finally, the evaluation should reflect more than simplistic satisfaction that the criminal behavior may have been thwarted. Included in the evaluation should be consideration of certain legal issues and prosecutorial goals such as application of Fourth Amendment proscriptions against unreasonable searches and seizures, admissibility of statements made during negotiations into evidence, enforceability of promises made by negotiators, acceptable use of electronic surveillance equipment, use of force, and media relations (Higginbotham, 1994).

As with any other official document of the police agency, the critique should be distributed through the chain of command in accordance with normal departmental procedures. Since the document will most likely be used in any prosecution of the criminal offender, it should be made available to appropriate outside entities such as the district attorney or other agencies which may have assisted in the operation. In addition, a copy should be placed in the departmental and unit personnel file of any officer involved in the incident.

Chapter Nine

THE THREAT OF TERRORISM AND TACTICAL OPERATIONS

The response to terrorism has largely been addressed from the perspective of a national defense posture. When the word "terrorism" is employed today, there is usually a misperception that the tactics, technology, and motivations reflect only the political climates associated with the Middle East and Northern Ireland. As a result of this inaccurate generalization, counterterrorist policies and procedures proposed in the news media and scholarly literature are often developed in terms of international relations and military responses. While domestic groups may have their philosophical and motivational differences with their foreign counterparts, their tactics and technologies are often similar. For example, the bombing of an Israeli kibbutz by the Hammas faction of the Palestinian movement and the Oklahoma City bombing share common techniques and employ similar technologies.

In the United States it is local law enforcement agencies that are required to assume the initial responsibility for responding to a terrorist action within national borders, regardless of the perpetrators' identity and even if an action can later be directly linked to an international conspiracy. Although cases may ultimately be turned over to a federal agency for follow-up investigation, the unmistakable fact remains that local police officers will have immediate jurisdiction at the initial and most critical stages of the incident.

A second point to consider is the fact that local governmental agencies, particularly police departments, are often among the first targeted by terrorists. This trend has been advocated by theorists from both extremes of the political spectrum (Marighella, 197; MacDonald, 1978).

151

Therefore, this chapter will be approached from the perspective of the involvement of local elements of the criminal justice system. Topics to be covered will be examined in light of how they would impact upon the actual participants in a tactical situation perpetrated in the United States and will describe the managerial preparation that must be performed long before a situation develops.

THE SWAT RESPONSE TO VIOLENT POLITICAL ORGANIZATIONS

American society has long taken pride in its tolerance and actual encouragement of political and philosophical discussion and dissent. Indeed, much of the success, growth, and maturity of the American systems of politics, economics, and criminal justice can trace roots to various instances where the continued acceptance of the status quo was clearly inadequate and inappropriate. But, while the domestic dissent taking place during most of the twentieth century quite commonly appeared to be spontaneous and loosely knit, the terroristic form of activism of the 1990s and the approaching millennium can be viewed as clearly more organized, disciplined, and regimented. This combination may tend to produce outcomes that lean increasingly toward confrontation with the police.

Despite our normative and often emotional reaction that terrorists deserve immediate punitive sanctions for their actions and particularly that any foreign sponsors warrant a military response, our political and criminal justice systems dictate that such actions must be construed as criminal behavior subject to application of the rule of law. Furthermore, since terrorist actions are criminal in nature, elevating the perpetrators to a classification beyond that of a criminal often may afford them an undeserved hero status and additional followers.

Terrorist groups may differ greatly more than in terms of philosophy and political issues. Smith and Damphousse (1998) suggest that they also differ in terms of geographical location (rural versus urban), organizational structure (cellular versus confederation), philosophical targets (capitalism versus taxation and national government), material targets (corporations with defense interests versus big government and societal/cultural minorities), and composition (inclusive versus exclusive).

The presence of these groups tends to place law enforcement in a three-fold dilemma. First, a watchful eye must be maintained for criminal activity while acting within constitutionally prescribed parameters. The key to an effective police response to terrorism is intelligence. However, police intelligence gathering without regard for proper procedures not only jeopardizes criminal prosecution but also can provide the terrorist group with popular support for its agenda. Also a critical component is having a good relationship between the police and the community in order to encourage citizens in the community to provide the police with the information that may result in appropriate advance intervention by law enforcement before a planned criminal activity can occur.

Second, law enforcement is required to protect the larger, nonviolent and peaceful elements of the community from the criminal activities of these groups while allowing normal functions of government and business to continue without interruption. To approach a condition resembling martial law is an anathema to the American conscience and would be considered unacceptably suppressive.

Finally, the police are also required to protect the terrorist group from backlash responses by other citizens to a particularly heinous crime. For example, the Oklahoma City Bombing Incident certainly generated such a possibility.

Beyond early warning intelligence, SWAT teams should involve themselves as much as possible with learning about the patterns of movement, the weapons preferred, and the tactics used by potential terrorists. They should also attempt to conduct legally authorized searches or arrests in a manner that will not result in a barricaded confrontation with multiple armed suspects. Accurate and current information about the daily movements, places of employment, and routes used in travel help achieve this goal. One of the SWAT team's most important sources in gathering such information is a well-trained uniformed patrol force.

RECOMMENDATIONS

A review of previous incidents strongly indicates that rhetoric that the terrorist group members intend to "shoot it out" or that they "will not be taken alive" should be taken seriously. Fanatical devotion to a cause, coupled with a high degree of organization, preparation, and practice make this kind of operation one of the most dangerous problems faced by law enforcement (Hacker, 1976). A well-planned effort to arrest the suspects would include without limitation the following considerations and actions:

- Well-prepared and solid warrants based on probable cause for arrest and search.
- Good intelligence gathering and analysis to provide accurate information of the group's strong points and vulnerabilities with the focus of the plan placed on vulnerabilities.
- Operational security will ensure that the plan of operation and time of execution are known only by appropriate law enforcement personnel. All outward appearances should suggest a "business as usual" routine of daily operations.
- The plan should be based on an assessment of assets possessed by the SWAT unit involved.
- If the SWAT unit has any deficiencies, these weaknesses should be corrected long before the execution of plans; e.g., the operation calls for more tactical personnel than a single SWAT unit can provide.
- More than one plan of action should be developed and tactical alternatives should be in place for immediate action if the basic plan fails.
- Once the SWAT team is in place, verbal efforts to obtain a peaceful surrender should take place.
- If reasonable verbal efforts to secure surrender fail, particularly those conducted by trained negotiators, the plan to enforce the arrest warrant tactically should be given strong consideration as soon as feasible. This approach has the advantage of preventing the criminal suspects from fortifying their positions and helps keep the factor of surprise and unpredictability in the favor of law enforcement. Strongly defended positions held by criminals with a categorically announced refusal to surrender peacefully increases the likelihood that the confrontation will result in an exchange of gunfire.

Notwithstanding the final point above, as in the previous chapter it must again be acknowledged that there is no single, all-inclusive, or perfect approach to conflict resolution. Since each extreme on the continuum of tactical options carries advantages, disadvantages, and consequences, the totality of each individual situation must be considered when making a selection. At one extreme is the belief that the plan to arrest barricaded suspects should not involve an extended "surround and negotiate" process. From this extreme, giving barricaded suspects hours or days to devise a response to what is confronting them is seen as an error. The Branch Davidian Incident suggests that, at least in some instances, an extended situation lasting for days may increase the likelihood of an "apocalyptic" ending whereby law enforcement personnel, criminal suspects, and uninvolved bystanders may be injured or killed. On the other hand, a peaceful surrender of suspects who had barricaded themselves and their hostages following an aborted robbery of a sporting goods store in Brooklyn, New York, took place after a protracted period of negotiation. In this case the negotiators recognized various psychological clues that the perpetrators were resigned to surrender so long as it could be done without losing face (Schlossberg, 1974).

It should be further observed that tactics which have been successfully used in the past are taught in recognized training programs conducted by legitimate sources such as the National Tactical Officers Association. These tactics will not continue to be successful if known by criminal elements and should not be made public.

The extremely sensitive and occasionally controversial nature of SWAT engagements with politically based groups at times tends to result in an increased level of active participation by command personnel at the top levels of the police organization. Command personnel normally possess a general authority to be present at the scenes of these engagements if only to serve in an advisory capacity to ensure compliance with general organizational policies and procedures. Again it is notable that command personnel may have received at most a cursory level of instruction in organizational expectations and the appropriate tasks of command associated with tactical operations. In some instances the command personnel may not have received any such training. Regardless of the rank of the police personnel involved, direct participation in a tactical operation solely because the criminal group is a terrorist group or controversial actually limits the quantity and quality of useable options.

Active participation by well-meaning but untrained command personnel presents an organizational and operational dilemma for the trained SWAT supervisor. On one hand there is an organizational obligation to comply with the directive of the top command structure, even when the directive is motivated by political issues or a desire to avoid organizational controversy. But, conversely there is an obligation to adhere to the standards of the industry.

This predicament can be effectively addressed by following two courses of action. First, all top command personnel should regularly attend intraorganizational training sessions to understand the abilities and limitations of the SWAT concept. This session should include a practical exercise in crisis management and should be conducted annually. Second, at the time of the tactical incident the SWAT supervisory personnel should prepare a list of feasible and appropriate options that includes the advantages, disadvantages, and consequences of each option. Ideally these options will be equally effective in the resolution of the situation. Realistically they will have different effects. In any case all options should be scrutinized thoroughly with particular consideration given to the consequences of adopting the option as well as the consequences associated with discounting it. Nor should an option be attempted under modification or compromise unless there is strong agreement on its utility, practicality, and likelihood of successful execution.

Once the situation has been contained, controlled, and de-escalated to such a degree that an arrest can be made, follow-up investigative strategies should be formulated to obtain a conviction. The arrest and follow-up investigation should be based and focused entirely on the criminal activities of the suspects, not on their political rhetoric or philosophical beliefs. Again, any other approach may unduly elevate the accused parties to an almost romantic and heroic status and may tend to hinder rather than aid the follow-up prosecution. Attaching a philosophical politically-based label to any criminal may tend to produce a martyr.

In Chapter Ten, the subject of tactical operations and the media will be discussed and a specific case history, that of the Los Angeles Police Department's 1974 confrontation with the Symbionese Liberation Army will be revisited. Readers are encouraged to consider that event not only in the context of the specific applications suggested in that chapter but also in light of the discussion points raised herein.

Chapter Ten

TACTICAL OPERATIONS AND THE MEDIA[1]

M ost Americans think they know quite a lot about police work, even though little of their exposure comes from direct experience beyond getting an occasional speeding ticket or reporting a traffic accident. Much of what is known, understood and misunderstood about law enforcement in the United States very likely comes from the media. American police activities are covered extensively on the radio and television and in newspapers and the movies. Whether the media depictions of police work are fictional or real, they can be compelling and dramatic, offering storylines that attract attention and engage the audience. The media depend on law enforcement to provide them with good stories, and law enforcement, in turn, needs the media to have its stories told. The police beat is highly coveted among journalists. Very often for television reporters, the beat is a high-profile position. News can always be found on the police beat; stories are just waiting to be told. And, because the public seems to have an insatiable appetite for such coverage, it should come as no surprise that crime-related stories dominate local television news. "If it bleeds, it leads" has been a catchphrase for years in television, and stations such as WSVN-TV in Miami, have taken the words to heart with a daily barrage of stories on murders, rapes, drive-by shootings, and stalkers (Marin, 1994). A survey in 1997 showed that local newscasts emphasized crime at least two-to-one over any other news story category (RTNDA Communicator, 1997). Even the major networks—ABC, CBS, and NBC—have placed more emphasis on crime news in the 1990s by tripling their count of such stories (*Broadcast & Cable*, 1997).

1. This chapter originally appeared in abbreviated form in an article written by Dr. Michael T. England of Southwest Texas State University and published by the Texas Tactical Police Officers Association in the Summer 1999 issue of *Command*.

This chapter describes the interdependent relationship that exists between the media and law enforcement agencies. Of particular interest is the relationship between television news and police tactical units. Later in this chapter incidents in which live news coverage exacerbated crisis situations will be reviewed with a reflection on the cooperative attitude that often prevails between most law enforcement agencies and the media. And, finally, recommendations will be offered for both the news media and law enforcement management when tactical teams are activated.

From old favorites, like *The Highway Patrol* or *The Streets of San Francisco*, to the current fare of *NYPD Blue* and *Homicide*, network television has had innumerable dramatic plots inspired by police work. This inspiration has often come from the actual files of law enforcement agencies.

The first program to take such an approach was Jack Webb's *Dragnet* —a hit series both on radio and television. Webb's character, Sgt. Joe Friday of the Los Angeles Police Department, was known for his no-nonsense, "just the facts ma'am" style.

Another popular series, which based many of its stories on actual cases, was the 1960s program, *The FBI*. Starring Efrem Zimbalist, Jr., the series had a loyal following, even among those at the highest level of the federal government. J. Edgar Hoover, the real-life director of the Federal Bureau of Investigation, was a big fan of the show. Hoover recognized the public relations value of having his agency portrayed as unerring and professional. Usually at the end of each episode, the FBI's "Most Wanted List" was shown to encourage public support for the agency's efforts to catch criminal suspects (Brooks and Marsh, 1985).

The FBI was a forerunner to the long-running series, *America's Most Wanted*, hosted by John Walsh on the Fox Network. This show openly solicited the public's help in locating suspects. Re-creations of the crimes were shown, along with actual photos, followed by graphics of a toll-free hotline to call authorities with information. The program's success can be measured in part by the many arrests that followed the show's broadcasts (Nelson, 1989).

NBC also aired a long-running program that helped police nab suspects. The series *Unsolved Mysteries* often focused on criminal cases in a fashion very similar to *America's Most Wanted*, with re-creations and actual photos. The national and international exposure of *Unsolved*

Mysteries worked in law enforcement's favor because the program would periodically highlight the arrests of people who had been featured in earlier episodes of the series (Nelson, 1989).

Programs like *Unsolved Mysteries* and *America's Most Wanted* fit into a genre of television programming called "reality based." The cases are factual but much of the visual representation of what happened at a crime scene is re-created. Actors and actresses are hired to portray the crime victims and perpetrators. They perform for the camera showing the viewers how the crime reportedly took place.

The Fox series *Cops*, though, offers still another angle on reality-based programming. *Cops* is unique because no dramatic re-creations are featured. It relies instead on police ride-alongs in which camera crews are allowed to follow police as they serve warrants, respond to calls, question victims and subjects, and make arrests (Katz, 1993). Ride-alongs are controversial because some criminal suspects, as well as innocent bystanders, have complained that allowing film and video cameras into their homes—with the endorsement of the law enforcement agencies—is an invasion of privacy (Zoglin, 1992).

A federal district court decision (*United States v. Sanusi*, 1992) suggested that law enforcement agencies concern themselves with privacy issues when they allow media access into people's homes. In the *Sanusi* case, CBS was forced to turn over videotape it had shot during a police search of a man's home after he had been accused of credit card fraud. The court decided the tape might be useful to attorneys and ordered that it be turned over to them.

The event that led to the Court's decision in *Sanusi* also spawned additional civil litigation aimed at both CBS and the police (*Ayeni v CBS, Inc.*, 1994 and *Ayeni v. Mottola*, 1994). Eventually the Second Circuit Court of Appeals recognized the possibility that the camera crew's presence constituted a Fourth Amendment violation because (1) the search warrant itself only authorized law enforcement officers to enter the home; (2) nothing in the warrant stated or implied that filming and recording which was unrelated to a legitimate law enforcement purpose could occur; and, (3) the whole purpose of the crew's presence was to enlarge the invasion of privacy needlessly by the potential for public broadcast at a later time (Emberton, 1997). This trilogy of opinions set out in great detail the specific concerns that these courts had regarding the practice of allowing the media inside the home during warrant service.

Kimberly A. Crawford (1994), writing in the *FBI Law Enforcement Bulletin*, concluded that: "If law enforcement activities take place where an individual has a Fourth Amendment right of privacy, media participation at the invitation of law enforcement is a violation of that constitutional right." Crawford urged law enforcement agencies to have written policies for dealing with the media to ensure that privacy concerns are addressed and to protect officers and their employers from civil liability.

The issues here were so serious that the United States Supreme Court eventually agreed to hear arguments in such a case and to rule on whether ride-alongs and subsequent media coverage are permissible or whether they are a violation of a suspect's right to privacy under the Fourth Amendment (Biskupic, 1999). Crawford's stance that in certain cases Fourth Amendment violations do in fact occur has now apparently been embraced by the Court, at least insofar as the media are allowed access into that most sensitive of all spots, the suspect's home.

In *Wilson v. Layne* (1999) the Court specifically held that bringing reporters into a private home during the execution of a valid arrest warrant violated the Fourth Amendment. Although the Court further ruled that the police officers sued were entitled to qualified immunity because at the time of their actions the state of this constitutional legal principle was not "clearly established," the *Wilson* case should achieve the result desired by plaintiffs in Section 1983 and *Bivens* cases aimed at state and local officers in the future who allow news and entertainment media personnel to accompany them into private homes for the purpose of recording and later publishing any sort of documentary information.

As to media presence at the invitation of police in less-sacred privately owned areas, or in public areas, the *Wilson* case, by degree arguably is not binding law. Also not addressed by the decision is any claim that a victim, such as a hostage or a noncriminal homeowner whose residence had been entered and barricaded, might assert against the media's inside presence with the police. Again, all case scenarios are fact-specific to some degree in the eyes of the courts. However, as Emberton (1997) stated in his analysis of *Ayeni v. Mottola*, "It should ... make a SWAT commander pause ... whenever he is contemplating 'facilitating' the filming of any SWAT operation." This warning notwithstanding, it is important to distinguish between filming, picture taking, or recording done by the news media for their ultimate purposes or benefit and that done solely by the police. If done by the police themselves in furtherance of specific law enforcement purposes behind the original issuance of the warrant (e.g., evidence gathering or a quality control effort to ensure that the rights of citizens are being respected during the warrant service) there would appear to be no problem. In fact, the Wilson opinion specifically makes allowances for police videotaping for these purposes.

Whether subsequent cases will expand this notion to other locations not so clearly identifiable remains to be seen. However, at present there seems to be no marked attempt by law enforcement agencies to restrict the media beyond the precise fact context present in the *Wilson* case. Both police and journalists, especially television reporters, therefore, have reason to pay careful attention to the legal ramifications evolving within the *cinema verité*[2] approach.

Ride-alongs are essentially an effort to be on the scene as events unfold, to capture the moment, and to provide information as it happens. Such efforts have long been the domain of broadcast journalism. In the tradition of Edward R. Murrow and his wartime colleagues more than a half-century ago, a goal of broadcast news is immediacy, and sophisticated technology makes it possible. With microwave relays and satellite trucks at their disposal, television reporters can routinely take viewers live to crime scenes. And, it must be understood that the media have significant constitutional rights of their own. The First Amendment gives the right to cover news from any location in which the public has general access (*Zemel v. Rusk*, 1965; Branzburg v. Hayes, 1972). The government cannot lawfully seize audiotape or videotape at a crime scene (42 U.S.C. 2000 aa). And the government cannot force a news organization to withhold information that it has legally obtained (Kirby, 1998).

However, going "live" to report news can be perilous, and invading someone's privacy is just one concern. Of greater importance is the preservation of life and safety. When law enforcement agencies deal with hostage takers, potential suicides, terroristic threats, and standoffs, lives are at stake. The journalist's goal is to get the story and report it; the law enforcement agency's goal is to protect lives. When

---

2. *Cinema verite*, literally "film truth," was a style of film making developed by the French in the 1960s. Directors used nonactors, small hand-held cameras, and actual homes and surroundings for locations. By the use of real people in unrehearsed situations, the filmmakers attempted to show life as it really is.

crises occur, the reporter may feel his or her effectiveness drained by the law enforcement agency's reluctance to share information. Conversely, the law enforcement agency may regard the reporter as obstructive if, in trying to get the story, he or she engages in behavior that jeopardizes the situation or adversely affects the preservation of the crime scene and the collection of evidence.

The Radio Television News Directors Association is the trade group and lobbying organization for broadcast news professionals, and the association's ethics code includes the following statement: "Respect the dignity, privacy and well-being of people with whom [news organizations] deal." The code serves as an ideal that some news departments occasionally fall short of reaching. Thus, the trend toward increasing media coverage of crime has its critics even within the broadcast industry.

Former police reporter David J. Krajicke, in his book *Scooped! How the Media Missed the Real Story on Crime* (1998) describes crime coverage of the 1990s as an unprecedented blood lust. Outside critics often blame the media for contributing to the violence on which they report.

The suicide on a Los Angeles expressway of a distraught man who was HIV-positive is an example. Viewers who tuned to local stations that afternoon saw on live television the horrifying end to Daniel Jones's life. News helicopters were hovering above the man to show the world his final desperate act (Stepp, 1998). Jones had sought the media coverage he received. Just before he turned a gun on himself, he unfurled a large banner with a statement protesting against health maintenance organizations. The letters were large enough for the camera in the helicopter to relay a clear picture.

In televised newscasts as well as in a commercially available videotape of the North Hollywood Bank Incident much more than the details of the event were shown. A review of the videotapes clearly showed reporters and camera crews in their zeal to obtain information from a closer vantage point becoming involved in the field of fire coming from both hostile and friendly sources. Movements of this sort can at a minimum be distracting to police officers attempting to focus on the criminal suspects, while the danger to media personnel exposing themselves to gunfire is obvious.

Police personnel have also claimed interference when news helicopters approached scenes where hostage negotiations were being conducted. The sound of a helicopter is deafening, and negotiators have on occasion had problems talking with hostage takers because of the noise. Some police departments have received assistance from the Federal Aviation Agency. Using a global position locator to determine exact longitude and latitude of the incident, the FAA can declare certain areas where negotiations or gunfire exchanges are taking place as temporary "No Fly" zones.

There have been instances where hostage takers have been able to watch police moving in against them—thanks to live news coverage showing the officers' positions. In Houston, for example, police say a gunman's reaction to live news reporting resulted in his death. The man had already killed his wife and was holding his two daughters hostage. He became agitated when he viewed television coverage of a SWAT team surrounding his house. The man fired a couple of shots, and officers felt that they had no alternative but to shoot him before he harmed the girls (Bardwell and Byars, 1998).

In another case, a wounded police officer was shown live on television during a shootout, and his family easily identified him and became upset as the event unfolded. For the sake of loved ones, the Los Angeles Police Department asked the news media to avoid similar live shots in the future (Lait and Braxton, 1997).

Recently on-air coverage of the high school massacre in Littleton, Colorado, drew criticism after a station chose to have its anchors conduct live on-air conversations with teenagers who were still trapped inside the school, thus jeopardizing their lives if the gunmen happened to be monitoring the broadcasts and found them. The anchors did suggest on-air that the teenagers seek help by calling the police emergency number 9-1-1 (Steele, 1999).

Journalists often take risks to get their stories, but the risks may seem indefensible when other people's lives are threatened by the actions taken by news reporters. Such a case occurred in St. Petersburg, Florida, when reporters for a newspaper and a radio station called a hostage taker and obtained interviews with the man (Holewa, 1998). News reporters are not trained to negotiate with people who take extreme measures; the situations are volatile at best and deadly at worst. In the St. Petersburg case, the hostage taker had killed a boy and three police officers before he took a hostage and later committed suicide to conclude a four-hour standoff.

Intense media coverage of breaking news events attracts a lot of attention, which is precisely what news managers are hoping will occur. Opportunity is knocking when police tactical units receive their marching orders, and few news operations can afford to ignore stories that offer the drama of lives in peril. If such stories are overlooked by one station and the competition covers them, the viewing audience can be expected to change channels to see what is happening.

Journalistic values such as importance, conflict, timeliness, and proximity are only part of the equation when judgments are made about which stories to cover and how to cover them. Also factored in is the potential impact the stories will have on ratings. Television news, after all, is a business commercially sponsored by advertising, and advertisers want to be assured of an audience. Even if live news coverage temporarily preempts advertising, the news leaders in terms of ratings will be remembered when buys are made.

Most television stations are fighting to survive in highly competitive marketplaces, and their survival is linked to attracting viewers. Live, on-the-scene news reporting is an element of television newscasts that, according to the market research that stations conduct, attracts and holds audience attention, especially when news events are breaking or unfolding.

But many news organizations recognize the pitfalls of live news coverage; they see the potential liabilities associated with being too close, too loud, or showing too much information. Snap decisions that must be made during breaking news events may be flawed, and for those caught in the web of a hostage taker or a terrorist, mistakes can be deadly. To avoid problems, some broadcast stations have adopted written guidelines to help them through their crisis coverage.

For example, the first rule for some television stations covering hostage or standoff crises is always to assume that the hostage taker or gunman is watching the televised coverage. Guidelines may also address police concerns about divulging information that might compromise the tactics or positions of law enforcement officers. The guidelines may also state, "Live shots should only be done if there is a strong journalistic reason. Ask if the value of a live, on-the scene report is really justifiable to the harm that could occur" (Cox, 1998).

Such rules in many ways mirror the guidelines issued by the Radio and Television News Directors Association, which were developed by Bob Steele with the Poynter Institute for Media Studies:

- Always assume that the hostage taker, gunman, or terrorist has access to the reporting.

- Avoid describing with words or showing with still photography and video any information that could divulge the tactics or positions of SWAT team members.
- Fight the urge to become a player in any standoff, hostage situation, or terrorist incident.
- Be forthright with interviewers, listeners, or readers about why certain information is being withheld if security reasons are involved.
- Seriously weigh the benefits to the public of what information might be given out versus what potential harm that information might cause.
- Strongly resist the temptation to telephone a gunman or hostage taker.
- Notify authorities immediately if a hostage taker or terrorist calls the newsroom. Also, have a plan ready for how to respond.
- Challenge any gut reaction to "go live" from the scene of a hostage-taking crisis, unless there are strong journalistic reasons for a live, on-the-scene report.
- Give no analyses or comments on a hostage-taker's or a terrorist's demands.
- Give no information, factual or speculative, about the hostage-taker's mental condition, state of mind, or reasons for actions while a standoff is in progress.
- Give no analyses or comments on the demands of a hostage taker or a terrorist.
- Keep news helicopters out of the area where the standoff is happening, as their noise can create communication problems for negotiators and their presence could scare a gunman to deadly action.
- Do not report information obtained from police scanners.
- Be very cautious in any reporting on the medical condition of hostages while a crisis continues.
- Exercise care when interviewing family members or friends of those involved in standoff situations.
- Make sure the interview legitimately advances the story for the public and is not simply conducted for the shock value of the emotions conveyed or as a conduit for the interviewee to transmit messages to specific individuals.

While these guidelines should be generically acceptable to police tactical managers, there are almost always more specific concerns that individual tactical managers may recognize through their experiences, or that a particular event may raise while in progress. Broadcasters in Portland, Oregon, Tampa, Florida, and Boston, Massachusetts, have worked out agreements with their local police departments about how live news coverage should be conducted. Boston's seven television stations and several of the city's radio stations have agreed to a "Partnership Agreement for Responsible Broadcasting." The document sets coverage guidelines during hostage situations. One result of the agreement was that no live pictures of the shooting incident at Columbine High School in Littleton, Colorado, were shown. Boston viewers who watched their local stations during the shooting were not able to see any live shots of SWAT teams entering the school, or of students running from the school, or of the news anchors interviewing the students trapped inside (Arvidson, 1999).

In February 1998, the four television news directors in Portland, Oregon, met with officials from the police department to draw up a cooperative agreement. The stations agreed to limit their live coverage in certain situations. For example, live reporting will be muted, according to the guidelines, when hostages are involved, when armed suspects barricade themselves, or when explosive devices are used. Also, no live broadcasts of tactical maneuvers can be shown. In return, each Portland television newsroom received a dedicated phone line connected directly to the police public information officer. Also, the local police agreed that when a crisis occurred, a pool camera could be used, and the law enforcement agency would assist in finding a suitable location for the camera (Moffett, 1998).

Cooperation between the police and the media is essential for both sides to do their jobs effectively and safely. One of the key components in maintaining a spirit of cooperation is for the police department to have an authoritative, responsible public information officer. Mike Cox, who serves as chief of media relations for the Texas Department of Public Safety, describes his job as making sure "the news media get the facts on issues involving the DPS and that the public stays informed, while at the same time allowing law enforcement officers to go about their business without me causing too many interruptions" (Cox, 1998).

The media relations director or public information officer is usually a news reporter's main source of information during a crisis involving tactical operations teams. His or her job is to gather facts and then report them to the media. Part of the role is to know what to say and what not to say when briefing reporters. Cox offers these "Silver Bullets of Good Judgment":

1. Avoid "off-the-record" talk.
2. Avoid flippant, glib, opinionated, racist, or sexist remarks.
3. Never say anything you would not want to see printed or broadcast.
4. Do not rely on "No comment."
5. Stay away from speculation.
6. Make sure your information is accurate—stay general until the information is firm.
7. Avoid using jargon.
8. Develop a relationship of trust with editors and reporters.

Trust is essential for law enforcement agencies and the news media to work together effectively. Trust, though, takes time to cultivate. The public information officer needs to establish ongoing relationships with reporters and photographers and their bosses. A place to start is by visiting radio and television stations, cable operators, and the newspaper offices.

Another component of a successful relationship with the media is to have standard operating procedures that ensure fairness, timeliness, and cooperation. Woodall (1998) suggests written policies are needed for police departments and their tactical units to establish procedures for "a positive and mutually beneficial working relationship between the news media and the agency."

Trust and credibility, characteristics which are both individual and organizational, cannot be established on an immediate or on a case-by-case basis. Building trust and credibility is much like putting money in the bank for a rainy day with each daily increment being of little significance or consequence but greatly appreciated on the day of reckoning. The process requires building bridges between the tactical unit, the community and all of the area governmental agencies. In order that there be no misunderstanding, speculation, misinformation, or inaccuracy in the information received by these entities, it is imperative that these different groups understand what the SWAT team is, why it was created, why it is an integral part of the police department, what it can do, and, equally important, what it cannot do.

Some departments have enjoyed a measure of success in educating the news media about these issues by including reporters as part of selected training scenarios, both as observers as well as participants. For example, the Detroit Police Department has occasionally used local television reporters as role players during disaster drills. The practice benefits both the news media and the police department, especially the public information personnel and the upper executives whose duties include regular and unscheduled meetings with media representatives.

As a rule, the chief of police should be the person to discuss the department's policies, organizational structure, general procedures, and organizational expectations of how police personnel should function in specific situations. In the absence of the chief, the public information officer, whose function is to expedite the flow of information between the department and the news media, will perform this duty.

Once the overall briefing is conducted, a ranking officer, usually the unit's commanding officer or a unit supervisor, should be made available to discuss the specific details of the incident. Whether the incident is a bomb threat, bank robbery, homicide, or barricaded suspect, neither the chief nor the public information officer usually possesses sufficient experience, expertise, or situational information to comment meaningfully on the subject. Under most circumstances a participant in the episode should not be put into an interview situation with the news media during or immediately after the incident. In many cases the stress of the event is still a real factor to be confronted. In most cases the final tasks of preparing reports remain unfinished. In all cases the participants have made life and death decisions generally under extremely demanding circumstances and without the benefit of assistance or consultation. These decisions are made with the understanding that they will come under intense scrutiny and that the facts leading to these decisions will require introspection, reflection, organization, and comprehension before further action is warranted.

CASE HISTORY: THE GUN BATTLE BETWEEN THE SYMBIONESE LIBERATION

ARMY AND THE LOS ANGELES POLICE SWAT TEAM[3]

Symbiosis is a word describing the blending together of dissimilar cells or life forms for mutual benefit. Hence the name Symbionese Liberation Army: the gathering together of radical students, convicts, men, and women of all ethnic backgrounds to murder, rob, and terrorize on a national scale. The SLA numbered forty-four members and had gained national and international attention when Patty Hearst, a young University of California student, was kidnapped by members of the organization. The Hearst family owned the Hearst newspaper conglomerate. The kidnapping was performed to leverage the group's demand that the family provide millions of dollars to feed the poor.

---

3. The abbreviated description of this event offered here is based largely upon the personal experiences and recollections of Ron McCarthy, who was serving as a Sergeant with the Los Angeles Police Department SWAT Team and as a leader of the so-called "rear team" of officers who engaged members of the SLA in that city on May 17, 1974. The Los Angeles SWAT Team's confrontation with the SLA is certainly not limited in instructional value to the area of media relations. Indeed, it may be viewed as fertile ground for discussions of any number of issues related to the management and operation of tactical units. This short version is aimed at being content specific to this chapter.

Throughout the early months of 1974 the SLA had been linked to several criminal activities in the state of California. Among the incidents attributed to the group were robberies, murders, and the attempts to take the lives of law enforcement personnel, including the placement of a bomb under a Los Angles police patrol car that was parked in a parking lot in Hollywood, California.[4]

Efforts to locate the group members were largely at a standstill until May 16, 1974. On that day SLA members were caught shoplifting in a sporting goods store in Inglewood, California. Their escape from the store, reported as being punctuated by gun shots from automatic weapons fired from their getaway car, marked the beginning of another crime spree in which the SLA was accused of carjacking two other vehicles. Later abandoning their safehouse on 82nd Street in Los Angeles, members with three vans believed to be full of guns, ammunition, and explosives vanished into the endless Los Angeles metroplex. When personnel from the FBI and Los Angeles Police Department subsequently located the empty safehouse, they encountered large quantities of ammunition and SLA propaganda left behind. The departure of the suspects offered the authorities no concrete leads for locating the elusive members of the group.

Nonetheless, officers of the Los Angeles SWAT Team continued to search the Newton Street Division areas of the city for any sign of the SLA. Eventually, as they moved through an alley within the district, they found the SLA vans, apparently abandoned. The vans were immediately placed under surveillance and additional SWAT Team officers, patrol officers, and investigators from the Department's Anti-Terrorist and Criminal Conspiracy Section descended on the area in an effort to contain any SLA members possibly remaining nearby. Interviews with citizens in the neighborhood disclosed that suspects fitting the description of the SLA might be occupying a residence on 54th Street. As a result, the residence was secured by seventeen members of the SWAT Team. Nine of those officers were positioned at the front while eight officers were deployed at the rear of the location. The tactical commander used the bullhorn and demanded that the occupants of the house exit. One adult male and one young boy emerged from the house in response to the order to vacate. While the adult

4. The SLA was resurrected in the news in June, 1999, when one of its long-time fugitive members, Kathleen Soliah, was finally arrested. Although she had assumed a typical upper middle class life as a wife and mother, her prior history had been the subject of a recent episode of *America's Most Wanted* (Chua-Eoan, 1999; Tortora, 1999).

maintained that the SLA was not inside, the boy contradicted this statement with descriptions of occupants wearing belts of ammunition across their chests with rifles and machine guns in hand.

Tear gas was fired into the residence after the rear team saw a refrigerator being pushed past a window in an apparent attempt to barricade the back door. The tear gas was met with a barrage of fully automatic and semiautomatic weapons fire leveled at the officers. Thus began a sixty-three-minute critical incident wherein public attention became riveted to the scene through live news media reports. In the end, all SLA members continuing to occupy the residence had perished despite the police calls for surrender. There was no loss of life sustained by bystanders or police officers as a result of the encounter.

Within the context of this chapter, the event has a special significance in at least one key respect. After the event, the young boy who had originally exited the house was interviewed by Los Angeles police officers. He disclosed that the SLA members inside had been alerted to attempts to arrest by the sound of news helicopters overhead, and that the resulting live television coverage was being viewed from within. This statement raises a specter previously appearing within the pages of this chapter; i.e., that of barricaded persons possessing the ability to monitor outside police activities and positions. To what extent that capability may have impacted courses of action taken by the SLA, much less the ultimate outcome, of course remains speculative. However, as suggested earlier in this chapter, there is an ample body of wisdom that the journalistic value of live shots must be carefully balanced against the potential for harm to human life inherent in compromising the tactics or positions of law enforcement officers. That risk is something that journalists should (and the vast majority do) fully appreciate in a general sense. But it remains constantly important that the tactical manager not only continue to remind the media of the general risk involved, but to further educate the media as to exact tactical strategies that may be compromised by instantaneous media coverage.

Chapter Eleven

NON-SWAT USES OF THE TACTICAL TEAM

A common misperception portrayed by the entertainment media suggests that tactical units are either engaged each day in a critical mission or merely staffing a basement office in a police station while waiting for the next tactical mobilization. For most police departments the issue of what to do with a tactical unit when it is not deployed on an actual tactical operation or engaged in a training exercise is not a major concern. Since most tactical units are part-time duties staffed by personnel who are assigned to other primary duties, the matter is very uncomplicated; i.e., the officers simply return to their primary assignments and perform the requisite duties associated with those posts.

For the relatively few tactical units that are full-time in nature, there has been an occasional need to justify the expenses of permanent assignments to elected politicians and appointed administrators. These units are found in the police departments of the larger cities and in some of the sheriff's offices of the more densely populated counties. The purpose of this chapter is not to provide a rationale for organizing in such a way that requires a permanent and full-time commitment of personnel and resources. Instead this chapter is intended to identify some of the other types of critical incidents that require a response by several officers for complete resolution without diminishing the ability of the law enforcement agency to respond to routine calls for police service.

SATURATION PATROL

In most instances criminal behavior appears to be random and spo-
radic and dependent on factors such as passion and opportunity.
However, an analysis of crimes committed in an area occasionally
identifies a pattern of activity that warrants special attention from the
patrol force. These patterns of criminal behavior may range from the
usually low-priority items such as traffic offenses to the generally high-
urgency offenses such as sexual assaults on school children.
Irrespective of the type of criminal behavior being displayed and
repeated in an identified area, its resolution often requires coordinated effort by several officers even when there is only a single perpetrator involved. For example, the arrest of Richard Ramirez (aka "The
Hillside Strangler") was the result of a specially created task force of
personnel from the Los Angeles Police Department. Many of these
officers were taken from their normal assignments on the SWAT Team
and directed to concentrate their efforts and energies exclusively in a
specified geographical area to effect the arrest of this lone criminal.
The task force used a variety of established law enforcement techniques such as surveillance, decoys, and finally physical endurance
and brute strength to chase the suspect on foot and wrestle him to the
ground. The availability of a large number of officers working in concert resulted in the arrest of an individual responsible for several
assaults and rapes in the Los Angeles area.

Similarly, a dramatic increase in the abduction, rape, and murder of
high school girls resulted in the rescheduling of duty hours for Tactical
Services Section of the Detroit Police Department. The increase of uniformed personnel not only resulted in the arrest of the perpetrator, but
also markedly reduced the rate of juvenile crime simply through the
deterrent effect.

In both cases the law enforcement techniques required the use of
several officers. In a form of selective enforcement, these officers could
disregard other requests for service directed to the police department
in order to concentrate on the task at hand. Equally important,
because of their assignment to the tactical unit, they were well accustomed to working as a member of a team effort unlike many of the
patrol force who had been encouraged to work more as individuals
throughout their law enforcement careers.

WARRANT SERVICE

Tactical units can also be used in the execution of arrest and search warrants. The Detroit Police Department's Tactical Services Section regularly assigns an officer to act as a liaison between the various investigative units and the tactical unit. This officer reports for duty approximately two hours prior to the arrival of the remainder of the tactical unit. Whether a warrant is for the arrest of a specified criminal suspect or the search of a premises for illegal substances or contraband, the use of tactical personnel to conduct warrant service provides benefits for both the tactical and investigative units.

First, the techniques needed for the physical execution of any warrant are similar to those needed to conduct an assault on a hostage taker or barricaded suspect. In both cases the entry/raid team must approach the area without arousing the suspicions and awareness of the suspects inside the premises. Entry must be made in compliance with legal guidelines established for such action. In so doing the entry is often made with equipment and techniques that require extreme physical exertion. Tactical personnel usually have worked with such equipment on a regular basis and have maintained the physical prowess to do so easily. The ability of the suspect to continue criminal activity must be quickly neutralized in accord with existing legal standards. The premises must be properly secured to allow the arrest of the perpetrators and the seizure of evidence.

Second, using tactical personnel to conduct the physical aspects of the warrant service allows the investigative personnel to concentrate on seizing evidence and taking custody of the perpetrators. The investigative personnel are generally more familiar with the items to be seized and the suspects to be arrested. They are trained in such topics as the recognition and proper retrieval of evidence without contamination. In addition they are trained in the various types of tricks and traps put in place by criminal suspects. They are able to put this training to its fullest and most efficient use when they are able to devote their entire energies to their investigative functions by relying on the tactical unit to perform the physical task of making entry and securing the premises.

Finally, by following an approach based on a division of labor, the chain of evidence is shortened for courtroom presentation. A simple chain of evidence is less likely to produce allegations of impropriety and misconduct during the judicial process.

TRAINING

For several reasons, SWAT personnel are ideally suited for the role of being a member of the organizational training staff. First, they regularly receive more training than the average patrol officers in order to maintain their individual and collective skill levels. This training is not only substantively more varied, it is also more intense and conducted under extremely close scrutiny and with high standards of accomplishment for continued assignment within the tactical unit. In addition, the training comes from varied sources and is conducted under widely diverse environments such as the classroom, the laboratory, the firearms range, and the actual conditions and locations of application. Consequently, these officers are exposed to many different teaching styles and can appropriately apply these styles according to the needs of the students.

Second, under the conditions for assignment described in Chapter Three, SWAT officers tend to possess more work-related experience than the remainder of the patrol force. Because they have worked with so many different elements of the law enforcement agency to accomplish their tactical mission, they are in an excellent position to recognize the training needs of the rest of the organization. More importantly, through their experience they are able to apply both the theoretical concepts and the practical issues of the training to the demands of reality.

Finally, tactical officers tend to be highly motivated individual. They tend to immerse themselves in the demands of their calling and take great pride in their performance. This level of motivation can result in a contagious enthusiasm for the job and can be an asset in serving as a positive role model for younger officers.

RESEARCH AND DEVELOPMENT

Whether conducted in a theoretical or in an applied context, the desired product of research is the expansion of the body of knowledge in a given area. From both an organizational and an individual perspective, SWAT personnel are also well established to conduct research in the areas of new equipment and techniques for many of the same reasons they are so well qualified to conduct training. First, tactical officers have regularly been exposed to the products of research and development more frequently than many other law enforcement officers. Many of their techniques and much of their technology comes as a result of a continuous effort to achieve the goals of the tactical unit's mission. As a SWAT unit increases its sophistication toward this end, its emphasis changes from weaponry to tactics (Dobson and Payne, 1982). Much of this shift from confrontation to de-escalation can be attributed to a refinement in techniques through research and by an increased application of technology developed for purposes outside the realm of law enforcement.

Second, because they are often working with other elements of law enforcement, they are able to recognize the research and development needs of these units from an immediate perspective. For example, the research associated with the use of sensory-enhancing technology which is used at the scenes of barricaded suspects can easily be applied to investigative units such as narcotics enforcement units. Similarly, the comparative analyses and experiments conducted to improve the techniques used to control crowds at disaster scenes can be applied to the movement of large groups of people at less hostile gatherings such as those found in parades and sporting events. The application of the research techniques needed for tactical situations to the rest of the law enforcement community is limited only by human creativity and ingenuity and by managerial innovation and discretion.

Third, SWAT personnel tend to be very highly motivated police officers. This motivation is manifested by a continuous zeal to improve as an individual, as a unit, and as a discipline. Whether this zeal is the result of a realization of the critical nature of their assignments or is a characteristic inherent among tactical officers is immaterial. This characteristic is readily apparent in national and state conferences of tactical associations when the attendees are seen learning about new products and exchanging ideas during the informal sessions. When this fervor to learn is applied to the research arena, the work product is greatly enhanced.

Finally, the high level of motivation to improve and to contribute to the growing body of knowledge found among tactical personnel can be seen by the relatively frequent enrollment of these officers in college and university courses. This trend has been particularly evident at the graduate level where the techniques of scientific inquiry and research are so heavily stressed. For example, one third of the students enrolled in a graduate management course at Southwest Texas State University were full-time members of the SWAT teams from Austin, San Antonio, and the Texas Department of Public Safety. To a person, each of these students has used the research techniques developed through graduate study to contribute to the body of tactical knowledge since receiving their Master's degrees.

INFREQUENT YET CRITICAL ASSIGNMENTS OF TACTICAL PERSONNEL

Some tasks in law enforcement occur on a relatively isolated and unpredictable basis. These tasks may include search and rescue incidents, dignitary protection operations, crowd control situations, and responses to natural and manmade disasters such as storms, toxic spills, and large-scale traffic incidents.

At worst SWAT units are used only for their primary mission, leaving the responsibility for the resolution of these tasks in the hands of *ad hoc* units. At best SWAT units are underutilized for these specialized, but relatively rare, assignments. For example, in 1992 during the mass disturbances following a court decision involving four Los Angeles police officers, the Los Angeles Police Department SWAT unit was used primarily for command post security when it could have been used quite effectively in a manner more consistent with the individual and collective experience, training, and abilities of its members.

These widely diverse emergency activities have several factors in common which strongly suggest that the law enforcement agency use SWAT personnel for maximum effectiveness and organizational efficiency in specialized task resolution. First, the relatively infrequent and unpredictable nature of these tasks require responses from police personnel who are flexible in their work assignments. The role of SWAT personnel within the law enforcement agency is generally defined in terms of flexibility with specific duties determined by organizational need. Thus, the use of SWAT personnel for many tasks which involve teamwork, structural flexibility, and focused attention is a logical outgrowth of their original organizational mission; that is, to provide the law enforcement agency with an ability to respond to extraordinary situations without detracting from its ability to respond to routine calls for police service.

Second, the dynamic nature of these incidents require response personnel to make unremitting adjustments to external factors which are usually unforeseen and unprovoked. SWAT personnel are specifically trained to recognize, analyze, and respond to continuously changing environments, both friendly and hostile. In so doing, they have already become familiar with many of the threat sources and have developed the ability to identify the available options and their ramifications immediately. The knowledge areas, skills, and abilities which had originally been developed for conventional SWAT operations easily can be applied to other areas of police service with little loss of efficiency.

Third, because of overlapping jurisdictional issues and problems of mutual concern, the safe and complete resolution of many of these activities require the cooperation of several law enforcement agencies. For example, a search and rescue operation could be conducted in a lake or river extending through several different jurisdictions. A Presidential motorcade could require the cooperative efforts of the United States Secret Service, the state highway patrol, and several local police agencies. The substantive nature of conventional SWAT operations occasionally requires mutual assistance involving the tactical personnel from several different jurisdictions. SWAT units already have the machinery, personnel, and logistics in place for operational cooperation with a minimum of effort. Potential or real friction can arise from the human sentiments of jealousy, contempt, or ignorance and adversely affect any cooperative effort among law enforcement organizations. Such friction can be lubricated through the familiarity brought on by the joint training exercises often conducted by SWAT units.

Finally, some of these activities require the same specialized equipment used in conventional tactical operations. For example, while SWAT units use rappelling equipment to place themselves into positions of tactical advantage, search and rescue teams employ the same equipment to move victims from positions of danger to locations where medical treatment can be readily administered. Similarly, responders to disaster situations utilize the same tools and techniques to regulate traffic as those used at the scenes of armed barricaded suspects. The expertise and confidence with the equipment developed through SWAT training can easily be applied to other law enforcement tasks.

CONCLUSION

To regard the development and maintenance of a SWAT unit as an unnecessary expense with only marginal and occasional utility would be a gross error of personnel and organizational management. If left to perform only in the capacity of its original mission, it would be an underutilization of resources as well as a waste of already completed preparation, training, and expenditures. However, if creatively planned, properly staffed, sensibly supervised, and functionally funded, it can perform its mission of providing the organization with a response capability without detracting from its ability to perform routine police tasks without interruption or diminished capacity. The SWAT unit also can be a definite organizational asset through its inherent ability to improve the delivery of police services in other elements of the law enforcement agency.

Chapter Twelve

TACTICAL OPERATIONS OF THE FUTURE

The authors do not lay claim to any ability for tactical prophesy. However, past events and current trends can provide a reasonable projection of likely scenarios and conditions under which tactical operations will be conducted in the future.

Like all other aspects of modern society, police operations in general and tactical operations in particular will be greatly affected by advances in technology. Equally important, changes in society, fluctuations in the economy, variations in political demands, and continuous modifications of law will also make an impact on police conduct. Thus, it is anticipated that there will be changes both in problems to be encountered and in approaches for resolution.

PROBLEMS TO BE ENCOUNTERED BY SWAT UNITS IN THE NEAR FUTURE

Increased Encounters with Juveniles

A review of the *Uniform Crime Reports* over the past several years may suggest a decrease in the crime rate among the adult population. However, a similar review would produce evidence that the tendency among juvenile offenders is the opposite. Several factors, sometimes working with and other times in spite of each other, may be considered in the study of causal relationships concerning this phenomenon. It is not within either the purpose or the scope of this work to offer explanations. It is certainly within the scope of this discussion to say that the likelihood is high that there will be an increase in encounters with heavily armed juveniles by SWAT units both in terms of frequency and intensity.

A particularly disturbing aspect of this projection is the observed increase in acts of violence involving multiple victims perpetrated by juveniles against other juveniles. These acts have been manifested through schoolyard shootings in Pearl, Mississippi; West Paducah, Kentucky; Jonesboro, Arkansas; and Littleton, Colorado. They have also been seen among the youthful participants in the fiercely competitive subculture of illegal drugs. Although each of these events appears to have been committed independently, a disturbing set of common characteristics has developed which may have important consequences for law enforcement in general and tactical operations in particular. First, the economic and social backgrounds of the perpetrators varies considerably. In addition, the geography of these incidents suggests that similar incidents can take place at any location. Aside from the fact that these juvenile offenders are often loners and do not appear to be from the mainstream of any one particular group and tend to display a fascination with unconventional and nontraditional teenage activity, there appears to be few generalities that can be offered for proactive consideration.

In a distressing application of "one-upmanship," these events have become progressively more violent. The challenge to copy and surpass previous episodes plus increased awareness of and access to the means of mass violence are very real factors with which modern law must cope. Through the use of explosives and semi-automatic firearms with large magazine capacities, fatalities have risen dramatically.

Finally, most young criminals surrendered to the superiority of responding police units in previous incidents. Tomorrow's youthful offenders may increasingly refuse to lay down their weapons and may show little reluctance to stand fast as a situation escalates into full-scale armed combat with the police. Whether such a tendency is the product of misguided juvenile feelings of invincibility and immortality or simply a reflection of rising overall societal violence, the police face a difficult dilemma. If the officers are forced into using fatal force against juvenile offenders, they may be characterized as overzealous and trigger-happy. If they respond with deliberation in an attempt to subdue and arrest the perpetrators, they may be criticized for being too slow to respond and uncaring about the perpetrator's victims. Irrespective of the action taken, the responding law enforcement personnel may be criticized more severely and from more directions than ever before.

Suicide by SWAT

Suicide is hardly a new phenomenon. As early as 580 B.C. when the poet Sappho is said to have killed herself over her unrequited love for the boatman, Phaon, troubled people have used suicide as the final solution to their problems.

Vexing circumstances and dramatic human conditions sometimes become subjects that require the action of police officers for resolution. Too often spurious theories, ill-conceived opinions, and incomplete research have forced ridiculous policies and impossible procedures on the responding officers. At times professionals within the ranks of psychologists, attorneys, and academicians have suggested that the police should have the skills to deal with the suicidal individual. At least they suggest that the police should be able to call a mental health professional to the scene to be utilized in some way to prevent a negative outcome. However, the availability of such a resource, at least on an immediate basis, simply does not exist for most police departments. What mental health professional is always available on Saturday at 2:20 a.m.?

Approximately 25 percent of all police shootings are "suicide- by-cop" cases (Hutson et al., 1998). More suicidal subjects have become aware of the phenomenon of law enforcement assisted suicide and how to create the situation they want for the responding police to use deadly force. Hutson and associates also found that 70 percent of "suicide-by-cop" situations concluded in less than thirty minutes. This time frame would obviously make it extremely difficult for law enforcement officers to summon professional assistance that probably is not readily available. Once summoned, it would be similarly difficult for the mental health professional to arrive, be briefed about the problem, move into a position to help, and exercise a meaningful impact on the situation all within thirty minutes from the time of original police contact.

In a completely independent study, Kennedy and associates (1998) agreed that police responders may become involved in shootings motivated by suicidal suspects more often than commonly anticipated. This study found evidence of probable and possible suicidal motivations in 16 percent of the 240 incidents collected and analyzed. By far, pointing or firing a firearm[1] at a responding police officer was identified as the precipitating factor.

1. In some instances these weapons were found to be unloaded. However, the responding police personnel are unable to determine this fact until the weapon can be secured from the suspect, usually after the threat has been neutralized and the suspect has been killed.

Various politicians, mental health professionals, and attorneys filing lawsuits against the police occasionally suggest that the police officers who confront suicidal suspects should use something besides deadly force to neutralize the situation. However, officers cannot be expected to accomplish immediate psychological evaluations and identify the mental and emotional problems leading to these suicidal incidents. Nor can they be expected to discover a solution to the perpetrator's problems in a few minutes when psychologists and psychiatrists who have given hours of clinical sessions to their patients cannot do so.

Conclusions can be drawn from these observations. First, suicidal suspects are aware of what it takes to generate deadly force responses from the police. Although the police are using deadly force with less frequency than had been the case ten or twenty years ago, the situations involving suicidal suspects have increased. This awareness extends to comprehensive knowledge about how to provoke a police response that will ensure the use of fatal force. It is not inconceivable for a suicidal suspect to seize a police officer as a hostage or even to kill an officer to generate a response from a tactical unit.

Second, the phenomenon of "suicide-by-cop" has managerial implications for community relations, post-shooting stress disorders among police personnel, and civil litigation initiated in allegations of wrongful death. These implications are far too serious and costly to be taken lightly and should be addressed in both recruit training and during continuous training sessions among veteran officers.

Acting by itself, the law enforcement element of the criminal justice system may not be able to address the psychopathological needs of suicidal individuals in general or victim-precipitated shootings by police in particular. However, through training, education of the public, and continuous research, the impact of this phenomenon on law enforcement can be assuaged sufficiently to allow its etiology to identify appropriate remedial and preventative measures.

SWAT Involvement with Weapons of Mass Destruction

In 1995 members of a doomsday cult employed gas in the subway system of Tokyo, Japan, not only for its immediate effect but also to instill fear among the population. Until that incident had been perpetrated, law enforcement had been relatively unconcerned about the likelihood of such an event and dismissed any threat no matter how little or great the potential for execution of the threat. Since that time the threat of an individual or a terrorist group using a chemical or biological device to cause mass injuries, panic, and long-term fear has taken on an air of reality.

Such an event could be catastrophic and only with a coordinated and cooperative response can the situation be managed. If such an incident were actually to take place, direct involvement by SWAT personnel may be unlikely. Representatives from fire departments, public health agencies, hazardous material units, and explosive ordnance disposal squads would be called on to neutralize the threat and to relieve any effects.

However, Hillmann (1999) suggests that SWAT personnel will have specific roles to fulfill in order to allow these other units to complete their missions safely and expeditiously. After receiving instruction in the basic principles of weapons of mass destruction and in Mission Oriented Protective Posture Equipment (MOPP-4), SWAT personnel should practice the physical tasks and communication techniques in this cumbersome gear because they will be required to perform several vigorous and complicated tasks:

1. *They will accompany threat neutralization and medical treatment personnel into contaminated areas,* particularly when there is a need to confront suspects and to control injured victims. This task will require sensitivity, the ability to convince victims to remain at the scene for treatment, and the ability to exercise an appropriate level of force for uncooperative and panicky victims who might otherwise contaminate the general population if they were to leave.

2. *They will provide security for these specialized personnel.* This task is not unfamiliar already. As irrational as the behavior may appear and as unbelievable as it may seem, firefighters and emergency medical technicians have often needed police protection when performing their own duties near disorderly, riotous, and frightened citizens.

3. *They will provide much of the labor-intensive tasks of identifying, seizing, marking, and preserving physical evidence* in such a manner that the custody and chain of evidence can be legally maintained for later criminal prosecution.

4. *They will assist with the evacuation of intended but unaffected victims.* It is safe to assume that these individuals, though not necessarily symptomatic, may require quarantine procedures. These individuals will

most likely be in a highly agitated and irrational state and will express a strong desire to either inquire about the condition of friends and family and to be elsewhere. The demeanor, expertise, and methods employed by police personnel will be a major factor in maintaining relative calm and avoiding an intensification of the problem.

CHANGES IN SWAT APPROACHES TO PROBLEM RESOLUTION

Creating and Maintaining New Standards for the Profession

A certain measure of creativity and modification are often expected and viewed as necessary for the resolution of the myriad tactical problems expected to be encountered by a modern SWAT team. However, creativity has its limits. The actual execution of plans must stay within the parameters of the rule of law, department policy, and standards of the profession.

New information is readily available through several different media. Attending the conferences of the National Tactical Officers Association and the various state tactical officers associations provides current information on the development of new techniques as well as an opportunity to view demonstrations of innovations in the technology. Equally important, these conferences provide association members an opportunity to exchange case histories and opinions regarding approaches to be followed under similar circumstances. Printed articles in professional magazines such as *Law Enforcement Technology*, *The Tactical Edge*, and *The FBI Law Enforcement Bulletin* furnish information on the newest developments in equipment and its most effective use. Academic journals such as *Police Liability Review* and *Journal of Contemporary Criminal Justice* provide commentary on relevant and directly applicable court decisions and legislation.

In short, a large volume of substantive information is available for the active learner in this area. However, too often the people aggressively seeking information about innovations within their respective disciplines are the practitioners of the art, not the managers of the organization. While there is certainly nothing wrong with practitioners possessing information, the amount of information and its dissemination is limited without organizational support and managerial initiative. Furthermore, operational-level personnel are generally not in a position within the organization to influence adherence to standards.

Modifications in Approaches to Training

Some of the future problems anticipated above, plus unforeseen others will require tactical units to incorporate a variety of new and innovative approaches to training. Instruction and evaluation both at the individual and the organizational levels has largely focused on the development and refinement of relevant skills and knowledge bases of immediate importance to the tactical unit alone. This traditional approach will have to be expanded to train jointly with other units of the police department as well as other public service agencies.

The expected increase in violent encounters with juvenile offenders and in the phenomenon of "suicide-by-cop" and the likelihood of encounters with suspects attempting to use weapons of mass destruction will usually require a response from more than a single unit of a police department. While traffic units have always been available to re-route or blockade pedestrian and vehicular traffic around the scene of a critical incident, the future problems will require a response from units with specialized additional areas of expertise. During the past two decades several police departments have developed support units that traditionally had been available only to the very largest of local law enforcement agencies. Such support may require the presence of police personnel from the victim services unit, the crime scene unit, the ordnance disposal unit, the juvenile unit, and the agency's legal advisor.

Future problems also suggest that resolutions will frequently require more than one organization. The trends toward incidents of greater scale and that often cross jurisdictional lines will require the cooperative efforts of several law enforcement agencies and support organizations. Some police departments automatically mobilize assistance from the local fire department and emergency medical services. However, the likelihood of incidents involving weapons of mass destruction will involve the Department of Defense, ATF, and the Department of Energy. The use of SWAT units to counter the epidemic proliferation of illegal narcotics activity will require close working relationships with the United States Coast Guard, Drug Enforcement Administration, Border Patrol, and the Customs Service. Situations involving the disruption or contamination of gas, water, or electrical service or any other large-scale problems concerning public health and safety will require cooperation and assistance from public utility and public health personnel.

Whether support comes from within the organization or from external sources, the possession of individual skills and knowledge is insufficient without coordination of effort. Similar to an all-star game where a collection of the greatest athletes is ineffective and relatively meaningless unless the efforts of the players become coordinated, the personnel assigned to specialized positions require coordination coming from supervised joint training and participation in mock disaster drills. Otherwise an actual operation may take on an appearance similar to the "Keystone Cops."

Conducting Continuous Research

To practitioners, the word "research" may conjure images of bespectacled scientists in lab coats and bow ties who may be geniuses in their respective fields but who often lack common sense and certainly lack real world experience. This perception may be due to the existence of theoretical[2] research for its own sake. This sort of research is highly esoteric with little immediate application and often very costly.

In reality, scientific research is an organized search for the truth involving problem identification, parameter definition, data collection and analysis, and the realization of a research decision. In a field such as criminal justice in general, and tactical operations in particular, applied research could address issues such as techniques, technology, and legal issues. While there may not be a legal requirement specifically mandating any form of research, the ability to display and document a continuous effort to find solutions for improving SWAT responses is certainly a helpful approach in promoting the image of any tactical unit and its management.

As an example, a tactical unit may wish to improve its ability to respond to barricaded suspect situations by examining the efficacy of various pieces of intelligence-gathering equipment or sensory-enhanc-

---

2. Theoretical research is also referred to as "basic" or "pure" research.

ing technology such as a thermal imaging surveillance system. Since there is a finite number of SWAT teams and a finite number of producers of this equipment, the definition of parameters for a population and a sample would be relatively simple. Data collection techniques could include experimentation, interviews, and direct observation. Data analysis could be quantitative, qualitative, or both. The research decision would very likely involve a recommendation to conduct follow-up studies on the most effective techniques for using the equipment during a tactical scenario. It would likely also include a recommendation to conduct further research on the issues associated with the legal use of the equipment.

It is a relatively simple matter to collect data through an examination of the physical and functional characteristics of the technology. However, to be able to analyze the equipment objectively may require external input. To document the data collection and to conduct the appropriate form of analysis would require more than a cursory knowledge of research methods and statistics. The level of intellectual sophistication needed to conduct this sort of inquiry properly is the satisfactory completion of a university graduate program.

The most obvious questions for organizational management are who would conduct such research and how much would it cost? By consulting the criminal justice department of a nearby university, particularly one with a graduate program, a tactical unit manager could easily find a willing and most able research associate. The faculty of these departments is generally composed of former law enforcement personnel who have also pursued outstanding academic credentials such as a doctorate or a law degree. Even if they are unable to assist immediately, they may have information on relevant research that has already been conducted. In addition, if the research problem being considered by the management of a law enforcement agency is important to a funding agency such as the National Institute of Justice, a grant may be available to absorb the expenses and to provide "start-up" money for the implementation of a conclusion and recommendation stemming from the research.

CONCLUSION

Extreme violence requiring a coordinated police response is a phenomenon with no foreseeable end. Most of the events associated with tactical operations are still committed by individual perpetrators as a result of either aborted criminal activity or personal psychological disturbances. Consequently, tactical preparations in the form of training, equipment, and tactical responses continue to focus on the individual criminal. However, a disturbing trend has been a growth in the number and strength of various well-organized criminal groups.

Law enforcement management will continue to be responsible for protecting the peaceful majority of society from those who would use the available opportunity and technology to further their criminal motivations. Whether the criminal is an individual or a group, motivated by economic gain or political and religious philosophy, rational and calculating or psychologically maladjusted is irrelevant. Law enforcement will continue to deal with these problems as they arise. The managers of police agencies will be required to anticipate these problems, develop proactive solutions, stay within a limited budget, and still provide routine services with minimal disruption. Of vital importance is the requirement that all of these tasks be done while staying within the rule of law.

The success of future tactical operations will require active and supportive management at the top levels. Success or failure will be highly dependent on how well this level and tactical unit managers can assess agency and community needs through scientific research, provide relevant training for police personnel, utilize current and developing technology from many different fields, coordinate both internal and external activities toward the achievement of agency goals, and objectively account for organizational performance.

REFERENCES

Abraham, K. S. (1997). *The forms and functions of tort law*. New York: Foundation Press.

Africa v. City of Philadelphia, 849 F. Supp. 331 (E.D. Pa. 1994).

Alexander v. City and County of San Francisco, 29 F.3d 1355 (9th Cir. 1994).

Alpert, G. & Smith, W. (1990). Defensibility of law enforcement training. *Criminal Law Review*, 26.

Arvidson, C. *http://www.freedomforum.org/professional/1999/4/23crisis.asp*.

Ayeni v. CBS, Inc. and Ayeni v. Mottola, 35 F.3d 680, 688 n.10 (2d Cir. 1994), cert. denied, 1995 WL 16587 (April 17, 1995).

Bardwell, S.K. & Byars, C. (1998, July 24). Media accused of Interference: TV helicopters covering standoff spurs meeting with HPD. *Houston Chronicle*, p. A37.

Beech v. City of Mobile, 874 F. Supp. 1305 (S.D. Ala. 1994).

Bennis, W. (1989). *On becoming a leader*. Reading, MA: Addison-Wesley Publishing.

Biskupic, Joan (1999, March 25). Justices question TV's use on raids. *Washington Post*, p. A2.

Bivens v. Six Unknown Agents of the Federal Bureau of Narcotics, 403 U.S. 388 (1971).

Black, H.C. (1979). *Black's law dictionary* (5th Ed.). Eagan, MN: West Publishing.

Blankstein, A. & Bernstein, S. (1997, March 1). Don't come out! Don't come out! *Los Angeles Times*. p. A-21.

Bopp, W. J. and Schultz, D. O. (1972). *A short history of American law enforcement*. Springfield, IL: Charles C Thomas.

Bowser, Charles W. (1986). The blood of children. *Temple Law Quarterly*, 59.

Branzburg v. Hayes, 408 U.S. 665, 92 S. Ct. 2646, 33 L.Ed. 2nd 626 (1972).

Broadcasting and Cable, Crime spree on network news (1997, August 18). p.28.

Brooks, T. & Marsh, E. (1985). *The complete directory to prime time network TV shows*. New York: Ballantine Books.

Byam, W. and Wettengal, C. (1974, September/October) Assessment centers for supervisors and managers. *Public Personnel Management*.

Chua-Eoan, H. (1997, May 11). Too many eyes in the sky? *Time*, 30.

Chua-Eoan, H. (1999, June 28). Hiding in plain sight. *Time*, 44–45.

City of Canton v. Harris, 489 U.S. 378, 109 S. Ct. 1197 (1989).

City of Winter Haven v. Allen, 541 So.2d 128 (Fla. App. Dist. 1991)and 689 So.2d 968 (Fla. App. Dist. 1991).

Cole, D. (1989). Tactical unit personnel selection in San Diego County. *The Tactical Edge*, 7 4.
Cooper, K. (1977). *The aerobics way.* New York: M. Evans and Company.
Cox, M. (1998). *Stand-off in Texas: Just call me a spokesman for the DPS.* Austin, TX: Eakin Press.
Crawford, K. (1994). News media participation in law enforcement activities. *FBI Law Enforcement Bulletin, 63*, 8.
Davis, J. (Producer) (1997). *North Hollywood Shootout.* MVP Home Entertainment, Inc.
Davis v. Mason County, 927 F.2d 1473 (9th Cir. 1991).
Dempsey, J. S. (1994). *Policing: An introduction to law enforcement.* St. Paul, MN: West Publishing.
Dipboye, R., Fromkin, H., & Wiback, K. (1975). Relative importance of applicant sex attractiveness and scholastic standing in evaluation of job applicant resumes. *Journal of Applied Psychology, 61*, 2.
Dobson, C. & Payne, R. (1982). *The terrorists: Their weapons, leaders, and tactics.* New York: Facts on File.
Downs v. United States, 522 F.2d 990 (6th Cir. 1975).
England, Michael T. "Media Relations and Tactical Police Operations," *Command* (Summer, 1999), *8*, 2.
Emberton, S. (1997). SWAT partnership with the media? Think carefully. *The Tactical Edge, 15*, 3.
Fine, S. A. (1974). Functional job analysis: An approach to a technology for manpower planning. *Personnel Journal, 53*, 1.
Fyfe, J., Greene, J., Walsh, W., Wilson, O. W., & McLaren, R. (1997). *Police administration.* New York: McGraw-Hill.
Gates, D. (1992). *Chief: My life in the LAPD.* New York: Bantam Books.
Graham v. Connor, 490 U.S. 386 (1989).
Hacker, F. J. (1976). *Crusaders, criminals, crazies.* New York: W.W. Norton.
Hale, L. T. (1995). United States v. Ford: The Eleventh Circuit permits unrestricted police use of thermal surveillance on private property without a warrant. *Georgia Law Review, 29*, 819-826.
Harper, F. W., James, F., & Gray O. (1986). *The law of torts* (2nd Ed). New York. Little-Brown & Co.
Hess, M. V. (1993) Good cop–bad cop. *Utah Law Review*, 1.
Higginbotham (1994). Legal issues in crisis management. *FBI Law Enforcement Bulletin, 63*, 6.
Hillman, M. R. (1999). Biological/chemical terrorism and SWAT response. *The Tactical Edge, 17*, 3.
Holewa, L. (1998, May 21). Media under fire for calling suspect during standoff: "It's a stupid thing to do. There are lives at stake." *The Ottawa Citizen.* p. B6.
Hutson, H. R., Anglin, D., Yarbrough, J., Hardaway, K., Russel, M., Strote, J., Canter, M., & Blum, B. (1998). Suicide by cop. *Annals of Emergency Medicine, 32*, 6.
Iacocca, L. (1984). *Iacocca: An autobiography.* New York: Bantam Books.
Illinois v. Gates, 462 U.S. 213 (1983).
Jacobs, J. (1983). *SWAT tactics.* Boulder, CO: Paladin Press.

Johnson, J. (1997, March 2). Gunfight fuels debate over police weapons. *Los Angeles Times*. pp. A-1,A-2, A-26.

Johnson v. Glick, 481 F.2d 1028 (2nd Cir. 1973).

Katz, J. (1993, January/February). Covering the cops: A TV show moves where journalists fear to tread. *Columbia Journalism Review, 31*, 25.

Katz v. United States, 389 U.S. 347 (1967).

Kennedy,D., Homant, R. & Hupp, R. T. (1998). Suicide by cop. *FBI Law Enforcement Bulletin, 67*, (8), 21–27.

Kerr v. City of West Palm Beach, 875 F.2d 1546 (11th Cir. 1989).

King, P. (1997, March 1) We were just trying to figure out how to stay alive. *Los Angeles Times*, pp. A-1, A-20.

Kionka, E. J. (1992). *Torts in a nutshell.* West Publishing.

Kirby, K. (1998, May). Avoiding the turbulence. *RTNDA Communicator*, 36.

Klingner, D. & Nalbandian, J. (1985). *Public personnel management.* Englewood Cliffs, NJ: Prentice-Hall.

Kolman, J. (1982). *A guide to the development of special weapons and tactics teams.* Springfield, IL: Charles C Thomas.

Krajicke, D. (1998). *Scooped! How the media missed the real story on crime while chasing sex, sleaze, and celebrities.* New York: Columbia University Press.

Kraska, P. B. & Kappeler, V. E. (1997). The rise and normalization of paramilitary units. *Social Problems, 44*, 1.

Laird, F. (1994). Infrared temperature measurement and imaging sensors. *Journal of Applied Sensing Technology, 11*, 8.

Laitt, M. & Braxton, G. (1997, March 1). Officials fear TV could show too much, too soon. *Los Angeles Times*, p. A-20.

Langford v. Gates, 610 F. Supp 120 (D.C. Cal. 1985) and 729 P.2d 822 (Cal. 1987).

Leovy, J. and Chu, H. (1997, March 1). In the bank, a huge monster in black yelled "Hit the floor." *Los Angeles Times,*m pp. A-1, A-20.

MacDonald, A. (1978). *The Turner diaries.* Hillsboro, WV: National Vanguard Books.

MacKenna, D. and Stevens, J. (1989). Selecting and training police tactical officers *The Police Chief, LVI*, 11.

Marighella, C. (1971). *For the liberation of Brazil* (Butt, J. & Sheed, R., Trans.). Harmondsworth, UK: Pelican.

Marin, R. (1994, June 20). Miami's crime time live. *Newsweek, 123*, p.71.

Mascolo, E. (1992). The emergency doctrine exception to the warrant requirement under the Fourth Amendment. *Buffalo Law Review, 22*.

Mathews v. Jones, 35 F.3d 1046 (6th Cir. 1994).

McCarthy, R. (1989). Command decision to shoot a hostage taker. *The Tactical Edge, (7)*, 1.

Mijares, T. (1993, Summer). Tower of lessons. *Command*. pp. 8-10.

Mijares, T. & Perkins, D. (Fall/1994). Police liability issues: Special concerns for tactical units. *Police Liability Review, 6*.

Mijares, T. & Perkins, D. (Fall/1995). Police liability issues: Tactical units and the use of specialized equipment. *Police Liability Review, 7*.

Mijares, T. & Perkins, D. (Summer/1998). Just like a Swiss army knife: the many roles of the swat trainer. *Command, 7*, 2.

Moffett, B. (1998, May). Turbulence. *RTNDA Communicator*, 32.

Monell v. Department of Social Services, 436 U.S. 658, 56 L. ED 2d. 611, 98 S. Ct. 2018 (1978).

Moon v. Winfield, 383 F. Supp. 31 (1974).

Mullins, W. (1997). *A sourcebook on domestic and international terrorism.* Springfield, IL: Charles C Thomas.

Mullins, W. & Mijares, T. (1994). Hostage negotiation in central Texas. *The Tactical Edge, 12 ,* 2.

Nelson, S.A. (1989, August). Crime-time television. *FBI Law Enforcement Bulletin,* 2–9.

O'Neal v. DeKalb County, Georgia 850 F.2d 653 (11th Cir. 1988).

Perkins, D. & Mijares, T. (1996, Spring). Interagency mutual assistance: the local government code and Texas swat teams. *Command, 5,* 1.

Perkins D. & Mijares, T. (1996, Spring). Police liability issues associated with interagency mutual assistance pacts. *Police Liability Review, 8.*

Perkins, D. & Mijares, T. (1997). Engagements with violent criminals. *The Tactical Edge, 15,* 3.

Perkins, D. & Mijares, T. (1998). Domestic law enforcement's use of sensory enhancing technology in terrorist situations. In H. Kushner (Ed.), *The future of terrorism: Violence in the new millennium.* Thousand Oaks, CA: Sage Publications.

Plakas v. Drinski, 19 F. 3d 1143 (7th Cir., cert. denied, 115 S. Ct. 81, 1994).

Price, C., Pollock, M., Gettman, L., & Kent, D. (1977). *Physical fitness programs for law enforcement officers: A manual for police administrators.* Washington, DC: United States Government Printing Office.

Prosser, W. L. & Keeton, W. P. (1984). *The law of torts* (5th Ed.). Eagan, MN: West Publishing.

Rivas V. Freeman, 940 F.2d 1491 (11th Cir. 1991).

Sager v. City of Woodland Park, 543 F. Supp. 282 (D.Colo. 1982) A-3 D/PS.

Salas v. Carpenter, 980 F.2d 299 (5th Cir. 1992).

Schlossberg, H. (1974). *Psychologist with a gun.* New York: Coward, McCann, and Geoghegan.

Schmidt, W. (1976). Recent developments in police civil liability. *Journal of Police Science and Administration, 4,* 2.

Schmitt, N. & Coyle, B. (1976). Applicant decisions in the employment interview. *Journal of Applied Psychology, 61,* 2.

Shuster, B. (1997, March 5). Wounded officer tells of his gunfight for survival. *Los Angeles Times,* pp. A-1, A-17.

Shuster, B. & Rainey, J. (1997, March 1). Officers face barrage of bullets to take comrades out of line of fire. *Los Angeles Times,* pp. A-1, A-22.

Smith B. and Damphousse K. (1998). Two decades of terror: Characteristics, trends, and prospects for the future of terrorism in America. In H. Kushner, (Ed.), *The future of terrorism: Violence in the new millennium.* Thousand Oaks, CA: Sage Publications.

Snow, R. L. (1996). *SWAT teams.* New York: Plenum Press.

Speiser, S. M., Krause, C. F. & Gans, A. W. (1983). *The American law of torts.* Eagan, MN: West Publishing Group/Bancroft-Whitney.

Starling, G. (1998). *Managing the public sector.* Fort Worth, TX: Harcourt Brace College Publishers.

Statchen, R. T. (1992, March/April). Defending 1983 police misconduct actions in the 1990's. *Federal Bar News and Journal.*

Steele, R. (1999, May 1). Journalism in tragedy's glare. *St. Petersburg Times,* p. A-1.

Stepp, C. S. (1998). The fallout from too much crime coverage. *American Journalism Review, 20,* 3.

Sterling, C. (1981). *The terrorist network.* New York: Holt, Rinehart, & Winston.

Stojkovic, S., Kalinich, D., & Klofas, J. (1998). *Criminal justice organizations.* Belmont, CA: West/Wadsworth Publishing.

Sykes, G. & Matza, D. (1957). Techniques of neutralization: A theory of delinquency. *American Sociological Review, 22.*

Tennessee v Garner, 471 U.S. 1 (1985).

Thompson, L. (1988). *The rescuers.* New York: Dell.

Tophoven, R., Verlag, B., & Verlag, G. (1984). *GSG-9: German response to terrorism.* Bonn, Germany: Neue Stalling.

Tortora, A. (1999, June 17). Suspected terrorist arrested in Minn. *USA Today,* p. 3-A.

Treusch, M. (1991). One level above SWAT? *Police, 15,* 7.

United States v. Karo, 468 U.S. 705 (1984).

United States v. Sanusi, 813 F. Supp. 149 (E.D.N.Y. 1992).

Urbonya, K. R. (1993). Accidental shootings as Fourth Amendment seizures. *Hastings Constitutional Law Quarterly, 20,* 337–388.

Waddington, P.A.J. (1990, October). Overkill or minimum force? *Criminal Law Review,* 697.

Walker, S. (1999). *The police in America.* Boston: McGraw-Hill.

Walls v. City of Detroit, et al., 993 F.2d 1548; 1993 WL 158498 (Unpublished opinion, No. 92-1846, 6th Cir. 1993)

Warden v. Hayden, 387 U.S. 294 (1967).

Wargo, M. (1989). The chiefs's role in a hostage/barricaded subject incident. *The Police Chief, 56,* 11.

What's in the news? (1997, August). *RTNDA Communicator,* p.11.

Wierstak v. Heffernan, 789 F.2d 968 (1st Cir. 1986).

Williams v. Denver, 99 F.3d 1009 (10th Cir. 1996).

Wilson v. Layne, 119B S.Ct. 1692 (1999).

Woodall, E. (1998). Why have a written media relations policy? *The Police Chief, 65,* 6.

Yukl, G. (1994). Leadership in organizations. Englewood Cliffs, NJ: Prentice-Hall.

Zemel v. Rusk, 381 U.S. 1 (1965).

Zoglin, R. (1992, April 6). The cops and cameras. *Time,* 62.

INDEX

Page numbers followed by t or n indicate information found in tables or footnotes.